P. Reutens

The Working Pit Bull

TS-235

Dedication

For my parents, Dan and Barbara, whose personal
integrity, kindness, humor and love nurtured in me my love
of nature, animals, humor and all that is right and good.
That was the most precious gift of all.
Thank you.

Overleaf: *Photograph by Isabelle Francais of an American Pit Bull Terrier.*
Opposite: *York's Bruno, a UKC registered male Pit Bull.*

© 1995 by T.F.H. Publications, Inc.

Distributed in the UNITED STATES to the Pet Trade by T.F.H. Publications, Inc., One T.F.H. Plaza, Neptune City,
NJ 07753; distributed in the UNITED STATES to the Bookstore and Library Trade by National Book Network,
Inc. 4720 Boston Way, Lanham MD 20706; in CANADA to the Pet Trade by H & L Pet Supplies Inc., 27 Kingston
Crescent, Kitchener, Ontario N2B 2T6; Rolf C. Hagen Ltd., 3225 Sartelon Street, Montreal 382 Quebec; in
CANADA to the Book Trade by Vanwell Publishing Ltd., 1 Northrup Crescent, St. Catharines, Ontario L2M 6P5
in ENGLAND by T.F.H. Publications, PO Box 15, Waterlooville PO7 6BQ; in AUSTRALIA AND THE SOUTH
PACIFIC by T.F.H. (Australia), Pty. Ltd., Box 149, Brookvale 2100 N.S.W., Australia; in NEW ZEALAND by
Brooklands Aquarium Ltd. 5 McGiven Drive, New Plymouth, RD1 New Zealand; in Japan by T.F.H. Publications,
Japan—Jiro Tsuda, 10-12-3 Ohjidai, Sakura, Chiba 285, Japan; in SOUTH AFRICA by Lopis (Pty) Ltd., P.O. Box
39127, Booysens, 2016, Johannesburg, South Africa. Published by T.F.H. Publications, Inc.
MANUFACTURED IN THE UNITED STATES OF AMERICA
BY T.F.H. PUBLICATIONS, INC.

The Working Pit Bull

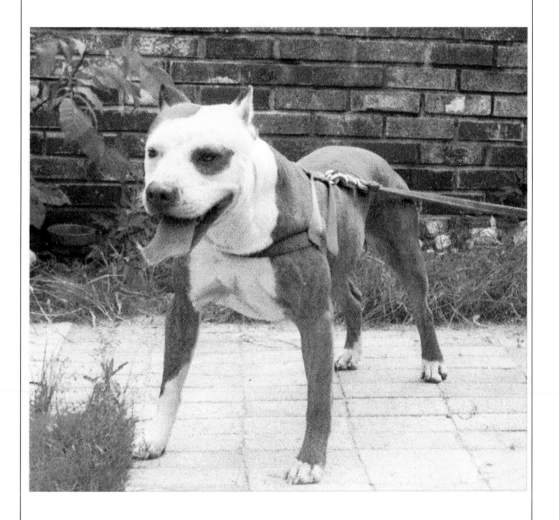

by Diane Jessup

Gr. Ch. Tyee's Satin Magic U-CD, at two years and Tyee's Blue Thunder.

Contents

Acknowledgments

Many people kindly assisted me while I was putting this book together. It is impossible to name them all. I would like to mention a few who not only assisted me in this endeavor, but whom I am also honored to call "friend."

People like John and Sharon Tatman, Ervin and Rebecca Gross, B.W. and Laura Lightsey, Joyce Klahn, Louis Colby, Mike and Dixie Lockwood, Marta Brock, Margery Malseed, Daisy and Charlie Holland and Theresa Beach. Special thanks to long time friends Mike and Judy Duncan, Theresa Ewing-Meadow, Carla Restivo, Virginia Isaac and Charles and Dr. Annetta Cheek. The dog game is better for your being in it.

Thank you Connie Patterson for single-handedly lowering my vet bill and anxiety level with good grace and humor, thanks also to Dr. Greg Bennett and the staff at Tumwater Vet Hospital and the Drs. Gilpin at Boulevard Vet Clinic for such wonderful care of the Bandog family over many years.

And special thanks to co-worker Joyce Marks, who saved my hide with the old "page down" trick, as well as caring for my animals when I travel, emergency proofreading, emergency computer instruction and just good old fashion friendship. And I must mention her dog "Judy-Judy-Judy," the miniature Dachshund, whom I consider a friend, and the only dog in the world to walk into my house and not only befriend Dread, but take away his bones. Also, I must mention the BOHICA's Dave Goldberg, Mike Verellen and Herr James Taylor, friends indeed.

Special mention to my family, ever supportive, my parents, sister Danene, brother-in-law Robert and brother Dan.

And of course, special thanks to my dogs; my family and best friends, who gave up so much play time with mom while she worked on the book. They are a constant source of pride, amusement, grey hairs and love:

The "A" Team

Ch. Bandog Dread, HC, B, WH, CD, TD, U-CD, U-CDX, SchH I, SchH II, SchH III, IPO I, IPO III, WD, WDX WDS, STD-d, STD-s, HTD-1, OFA

Bandog Brittania, HC, U-CD, SchH A, SchH I, WD, WDX, WDS,

Bandog Bad, HC, HTD-1, WD, WDX, (deceased) and Bandog Thriller, HC.

The "B" Team

Grip, the Pit Bulldog, Odin, the Doberman, Danger, the Rottweiler, and Roman, the Neapolitan Mastiff.

About the Author

Diane Jessup is the director of the Canine Aggression Research Center, an education and research facility in Olympia, Washington. The Center operates as an international consulting service to animal control and law enforcement agencies as well as public utilities and other public services on matters of canine/human interaction. The Center offers expert witness services for court cases as well as written and video educational material. She also works full time as an animal control officer in Olympia. Diane and her Pit Bulldogs travel extensively while giving seminars on dangerous dog behavior, as well as a seminar for law enforcement personnel on illegal dog and cock fighting.

Diane and her four Pit Bulldogs have competed extensively in organized dog sports, and Bandog Dread holds the honor of earning titles in more areas of dog sports than any other dog of any other breed. Dread, Brittania, Bad and Thriller hold titles in herding, Schutzhund, tracking, obedience, weight pulling, conformation, and guard work as well as having been used in TV commercials, five major motion pictures and several public service pieces. While working in the seminars the dogs have appeared in dozens of news stories as well as on CNN News.

Today Diane and her dogs are actively competing in dog sports and they enjoy each other's company while gardening and hiking. "The Village" as Diane calls her acre, houses the four dogs, a cat, about 30 free-roaming guinea pigs, a few dozen purebred bantams and a few Old English gamecocks.

The author with her beloved Bulldog family, Thriller, Brittania, Bad, and Ch. Dread, SchH III.

PR Tyee's Major Blue owned by Pamela and David Wofford.

Preface

In the mid 1980s I watched with horror as the Pit Bulldog was swept up in a fad panic, crucified by the press, the national humane societies, the American Kennel Club, law makers, city and county council members and thousands of others who certainly should have known better. Article after article, news story after news story, all were unfair, biased and sensationalized. How the dogs ever survived that time is a testimony to the breed's gameness and ability to inspire loyalty in its owners.

I sit high on a very narrow fence; I am not only an animal control officer but a professional consultant to hundreds of law–enforcement, public utilities and animal-control agencies across

The Pit Bull has been unfairly judged as an untrustworthy dog in the last few years. Here, "Spartagus," a typically friendly bulldog, sits with Kim Herron.

North America on the issue of dangerous dog behavior. Dog aggression is my business, and I know my business. I have no time for "experts" on either side of the Pit Bull "wars" who have no practical experience with canine aggression, who try and speak on matters of the Pit Bull's character. The Pit Bull is not a sheep in wolf's clothing, neither is he a wolf in sheep's clothing. He is a BULLDOG, with all the resulting pros and cons. On the other side of that fence I straddle is my "other self," that self which is an avid lover of Old English game fowl and Pit Bulldogs. Many people are confused by this seeming contradiction, they have come to associate anyone who works in the "humane" field to be somehow "against" the game breeds. For myself nothing could be further from the truth. I love game animals with a passion, yet I work just as passionately to preserve these animals from those who would exploit their character. I work to save the cock and the Bulldog from the fighter, for his actions now threaten these animals with extinction instead of preservation, and because it is not right that a man have an animal do his fighting for him. I also fight to save the cock and the Bulldog from the "humaniacs," such as PETA and other groups who would destroy them in the name of humanity without ever coming to understand the animals they seek to destroy. The world would be a far poorer place if suddenly bereft of the Bulldog's loyalty and power, and the game cock's beauty and pride.

I believe that game animals can be preserved. But that is because my definition of game includes a

This child senses a safe, loving companion while adults might let their prejudice cause them to fear this dog.

The Pit Bull grin.

wider scope than those who enjoy watching animals destroy each other. To me "game" means willing to try with an effort which is beyond the norm. You can be game without being aggressive, and so can an animal. The game animals have a special appeal, and they appeal to a lot of people, not just that small, sadistic minority which allow animals to do their fighting for them. The appeal of the game animal is his cocky, confident, friendly manner, and his "never say never" attitude. His aggression, when called upon, is spectacular, but no less so than his greatness of heart.

What amazed me more than any one thing I saw happen during the 1980s Pit Bull "fad panic" was the fact that Pit Bull fanciers were some of the breed's worst enemies! Most went about breeding litter after litter in the midst of the worst overpopulation problem our breed had ever known. Some even went so low as to promote the breed as an attack dog, which really put the fat on the fire. Some (usually those with puppies to unload) began to tell everyone that the Pit Bull was a sheep in wolf's clothing, a generic type dog which was really no different from a Golden Retriever. This was unfair to the dog, the dog's new owners and the public. Bulldogs are determined, rugged, intelligent animals which require much the same attributes in their owners. They are not "pet" dogs in the sense that this is what they have been bred for generations.

They have been bred for rough stockwork, but they have also been bred for common sense in family situations.

Others went about stating that Pit Bulls were good dogs, and misunderstood, but for all that they were still primarily good only for fighting. The dog-fighting "fanciers" were almost single-handedly responsible for getting our breed outlawed in several cities. They presented the dogs as super-dogs, extra strong and tough. Several books were published presenting an image of the Pit Bull as an animal primarily kept on a ridiculously heavy chain and fought for sport. These books left the reader with the impression that the breed was not really a house pet at all, but an animal which was best kept out on a chain and not really, somehow, capable of being trained

The Pit Bull's natural instinct is protection, not destruction, of their young friends. Owner, Theresa Beach.

"Sam," owned by Virginia Isaac, on the cover of a Sunday supplement.

like other dogs. I couldn't believe what I was seeing. Then these "pro-Pit Bull" books began being used *against* the breed in almost every court case in the country. I was involved in several of these legal battles and it was difficult and embarrassing to have to argue the facts against the false image put forth by other Pit Bull "experts"! At that point I felt what was really needed was a book which showed the Pit Bulldog as he really is, the majority of them anyway.

The books available when I sat down to write this either presented the Bulldog as a mindless fighting animal kept on huge chains and in sloppy, drafty dog houses by beer guzzling low lifes, or showed the American Staffordshire Terrier as a mindless show dog posing demurely on the end of a little string. These two extremes represent a minute percentage of Pit Bulls out in the world today. At any given time in the United States, less than 250 Pit Bulls are being shown with any regularity. At any given time, less than 250 Pit Bulls are being fought with any regularity. What are the rest doing? That is what this book is about. It's about what the rest of the thousands of Pit Bulls and Am. Staffs out there are doing.

I feel I can speak with authority on the Pit Bulldog. I am not a breeder; there are far too many dogs on this earth right now without me adding more, and as long as my job at the animal shelter requires that I kill a dozen or so healthy dogs every day (about half of them purebred, and many of them American Pit Bull Terriers), I cannot justify breeding more. I am a some-time trainer, a Bulldog historian, and a "behaviorist" (though I hate that word, it conjures up images of overpriced dog trainers calling themselves "dog pyschologists"). I have accomplished things with Pit Bulls others before me have not done. I have accomplished things with Pit Bulls which "experts" on both sides of the issue said could not be done. I understand the Bulldog, and because I understand him I have come to admire and love him.

Dread and I have done our little part to help the breed through its hard times. I watch with great satisfaction as others now work to beat Dread's record of being titled in more areas of endeavor than any other dog of any other breed. Dread never received much publicity about his accomplishments, I think

All set for the Fourth of July parade!

Taylor's Mr. Brown, from Sarona kennels.

Red Banner, a beautiful red nose/red pup bred by Diane Large.

Are Pit Bulls untrustworthy around other animals? This Pit Bull bitch accepts a baby raccoon and raises it as her own. There's your answer! Owner, Barbara Large.

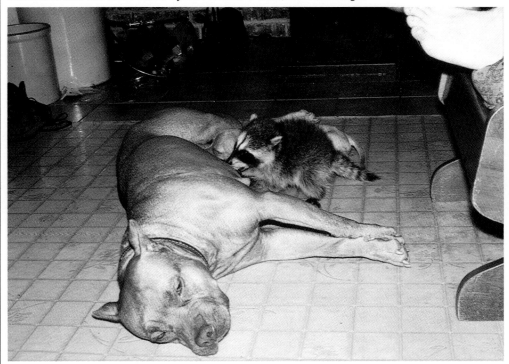

A nice whelping box. This plastic wading pool keeps drafts off the pups. Here "Rosie" has her work cut out for her.

Is this the face of a killer dog? A gorgeous red nose/red Pit Bull pup.

Sarona Big Eddie, a dog of almost perfect conformation. This is what a Pit Bulldog should look like.

Virginia Isaac's "Sam" proudly carries the flag up the tower on the challenge agility course.

respectable dog. But a Bulldog did do it, and it is my heartfelt hope that a whole line of Bulldogs will keep the tradition alive. I know Dread's record will fall, and I know it will be a Pit Bulldog that does it. My satisfaction comes from knowing that it is just this trying to overcome goals which will keep the Bulldog alive. When it happens it will affirm that the breed is alive and well and right on course.

I hope this book awakens interest in others to keep using the Bulldog for a variety of tasks, and to keep him working his springpole. I hope it interests people to keep him probably because it was too hard for the dog fancy to take— an old Bulldog doing that instead of some beautiful, full-coated collie or shepherd dog. Some rugged, tough, humble and goodhearted. I hope it helps people interested in learning the truth about the breeds to find that he is, like every thing in life, neither

A Pit Bull and her friend share an intimate moment.

PR Cheek's Red Baroness, U-UD, SchH III set the Schutzhund world on its ear by going to the Nationals and competing strongly. She was the smallest dog there and the only one to knock the decoy down. Owner, Annetta Cheek.

all good nor all bad. He is just a dog which tries very hard to please his master, and sometimes his master is good, and sometimes his master is bad.

As I write these words I look out the window at a peaceful evening; the yard is filled with 30 guinea pigs which are grazing in little herds all around the dogs. Bad, Brittania and Thriller are out there chewing bones in the middle of the yard, enjoying the rare winter sunshine. They are house dogs, but they also enjoy their time outside. Some game fowl and banties watch the dogs, waiting for a stray piece of lard to fall off the bones. Dread, an old dog now, lies on my bed sound asleep. In a week he and I will be off, all the way across the country, so he can be used in a movie being filmed in Boston by 20th Century Fox. It is his fifth movie, and the studios like to use him because like so many of his breed he is so intelligent and stable. He has been trusted to do bite work with several really big stars, and sometimes I stop and think, "what if a dog fighter had gotten him as a puppy—what an incredible waste of a dog. Or what if he had been born in a city with a breed-specific law which required his death at the hands of the animal control?" Either fate would have been tragic. Either fate would have deprived the world of a really nice dog. And I hope this book, in its way, will help to save Bulldogs from either of these fates.

Diane Jessup
"The Village"
Olympia, Washington

Who says Pit Bulls don't get along with other pets? These two friends cuddle on a cold Colorado night.

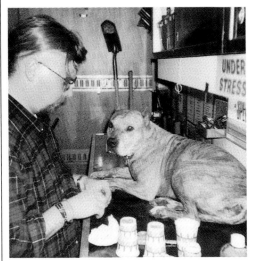

Dread getting his makeup job on the set of "The Good Son."

Gr. Ch. PR Guerra's Beringer, BH. CGC, U–CD, and his best friend Emily.

Dread and the author on location of the film "Getting Even with Dad."

This bulldog proves the versatility of the breed by herding sheep. He not only competed in sanctioned herding trials, he often won prizes!

"bulldog" when man began to rely upon domestic animals for food. They were used extensively to control cattle during the Middle Ages, and in appearance were identical to a modern Pit Bulldog of about 45 to 65 pounds. The function of these dogs, that of gripping and controlling cattle and bulls, was developed into a sport of sorts, both for the entertainment of the public, and a means of determining which was the best Bulldog. Bull-baiting became so popular that laws were written forbidding the sale of bull flesh unless the animal had been baited prior to its death. Later still, the breed's strength and courage were pitted against animals of all types, and eventually the dogs were turned against each other in the brutal and senseless "sport" of dog fighting.

The basic versatility of the breed was such that while some members were used for the fighting sports, many others were hard at work on farms and pioneer homes, still employed at their original work as cattle dogs, hunters, and guardians. "Jack," the brindle Bulldog mentioned in Laura Ingalls Wilder's famous *Little House on the Prairie* books, was just such a dog. Jack protected Laura from wolves, Indians and other frontier dangers. "Old Yeller" was another example of a dog whose Pit Bull blood showed through in the way he controlled runaway cattle by gripping them on the nose and flipping them.

Today the American Pit Bull

Terrier (or Bulldog as we shall rightfully call him) is still an active working breed, dominating weight classes at weight-pulling contests, achieving highest scoring dog in trial at Schutzhund trials (civilian police dog trials), earning obedience and tracking degrees, working in search and rescue, competing in sanctioned herding trials, working cattle on farms, working as "catch dogs" for those who hunt pigs, and working as registered Therapy dogs in nursing homes all across America. In addition to his use as a working dog, the Bulldog is still one of the finest family pets available today.

The nature of the Pit Bull is

Laura Lightsey with her famous SAR Pit Bulldog.

Fonseca's Spot, hooked to a land cart, is ready to pull.

How many dogs have you seen climbing trees? It's no problem for the athletic Pit Bull.

typical of all the members of the "Bulldog" family, of which he is the foundation. They are extremely outgoing puppies, friendly, playful and brave. As adults they are happy dogs, gentle with humans and friendly animals, but always ready to test their mettle against any aggressive animal. They make ideal companions for intelligent, experienced dog owners who want a little something extra in a dog. They require little in the way of grooming or special care, but because of their strong working drives absolutely require a well-fenced yard, responsible owners and plenty of exercise. They are house dogs, doing best if allowed to be a member of the family. They are very unhappy if abandoned to life on a chain, or forced to live in a kennel or shipping crate, as is so often done with dogs these days. They are easily taught house manners and shed very little.

The Bulldog is an extremely strong, robust dog and enjoys a stiff daily walk or time spent being played with in the yard. Children and Bulldogs are a natural, but like members of any breed, they should not be left unattended with children who may mistreat them. Well-bred Bulldogs are less likely to snap or become aggressive with abusive children due to their kind nature and rugged constitution, but children can be unfair, and a dog needs protection sometimes!

Becoming a Bulldog owner opens up a whole new world of

dog sports, from the exciting world of competition weight pulls to the highly complex and rewarding Schutzhund title. The Pit Bull owner, however, may decide just to enjoy owning a Bulldog for the fun he can have in his own backyard, inventing games of his own. Whichever course you take, owning a Bulldog is unlike owning any other breed. No other dog offers such a clean, intelligent, strong, brave, playful, protective, loyal, versatile and fun companion in such a compact size.

Above: Dread shows the full-mouth bite favored in Schutzhund. Below: A Pit Bulldog charges through the obstacle course.

Actually, the Molossus (early Mastiff) and the Bullenbeisser (Bull-biter or Bulldog) were two distinctly different breeds within a type. Molossus refers to a large mastiff-type dog, and is a very old name, a name which in fact can be found going back into farthest antiquity. Early references to Molossus dogs make mention of the dog's appearance, such as the Roman poet Claudian mentioning the area, but I believe that any attempt to trace any dog general/type to one specific location is doomed to failure. Certain early references were made to huge, fierce hunting mastiffs in early England, what is now northern Europe, through most of the Middle East and certainly in Roman territories. Some people have stated that the dog we now know as the English Mastiff probably

A very old German postcard showing early Boxers, which indicates how closely related they are to the original Pit Bulldog.

"broad-mouthed" dogs of England. Molossus refers to a type, as there were many variations of large, mastiff-type dogs that were all called molossus. There are many speculations as to where the type may have first originated, and some very early references are made to "Alans" or "Alaunts" coming from the Chinese steppe originated from the Neapolitan Mastiffs of Italy, yet the Romans imported Mastiffs from England to fight in the arenas. Huge Molossi were certainly known at that time in Italy, so it appears that there was already a certain number of Molossus varieties.

The history of the Bullenbeisser is very difficult to separate from the Molossus, and in fact, to this day the two types are still more similar than not, but early references to the separation of the two types are apparent. Edward, the Second Duke of York, describes the different varieties of "Alaunts," and makes reference to the "Alaunt of the Butcheries." This name literally translates as "Mastiff-Butcher's Dog" or "Mastiff-Bulldog" thus giving life to the idea that perhaps the Bullenbeisser sprang directly from the Molossus.

The "Mastiff-Bulldog" is then referred to as an excellent bullbaiter, and further as an excellent boar dog, thus giving us the first hint that the German Mastiff, or Great Dane, a dog which quite clearly shows Mastiff and Bulldog traits, is also a direct descendant of the Molossus/Bullenbeisser. In the year 1631, the first real proof of the division of the two types is found in a letter from Prestwich Eaton to George Willingham of London. In this letter Eaton requests that he be sent *"a good Mastive dogge"* and adds *"pray procuer mee two good Bulldogs."* The Bullenbeisser (bull-biter) went on to become the butcher's dog, or Bulldog, a smaller, more agile animal that could work all day, and move quickly around cattle to avoid being kicked. The term Bullenbeisser, or Bulldog, should not be confused with the modern-day AKC-registered Bulldog. This is a recently developed show breed which has never been capable of work of any form. "Bulldog" is a

Oh Boy! Can't he fight

Circa World War I. America represented by the Pit Bulldog—the symbol of courage.

descriptive term, much like "gundog," or "coonhound"; it can describe a dog of one of several breeds which all perform a certain work. All manner of dogs, as long as they were stocky, tenacious, courageous, agile and able to perform the duties of a butcher's dog, were called "Bulldogs." The modern American Kennel Club "show Bulldog" is not a functional breed, and should therefore, ironically, not be considered a true "Bulldog." The only direct descendant of the original Bullenbeisser, very little changed, is the modern American Pit Bull Terrier (erroneously called a terrier).

started from: a Molossus/ Bullenbeisser cross. These are the Bullmastiff, an obvious cross between the Bulldog and the Mastiff, and the Great Dane, developed from large, aggressive Bullenbeissers, which by virtue of their size obviously had Mastiff (Molossus) blood in them.

Of all the breeds descended from the proud Molossus and Bullenbeisser, only the Pit Bulldog and the Rottweiler are still used as working dogs to any real degree. Today the Boxer, Great Dane, all the mastiffs and the show Bulldog breeds are bred primarily for conformation points and show ribbons. The Rottweiler, a descendant of the Molossus, is used today in increasing numbers as a police and guard dog, much as its ancestors were used. Regardless of whether one approves of all the uses man has found for the Bulldog through the ages, one must look with admiration upon these dogs whose proverbial courage and tenacity represent the last vestige of the ancient Bullenbeisser.

THE WORK OF A BUTCHER'S DOG

Many people assume that the Bulldog was developed around the "sport" of bullbaiting, when in reality the "sport" was developed around the unique job of the Bulldog. It is hard for a modern person today to think

A print from the early 1880s showing a farm Pit Bull. The breed has changed very little over the years.

A very old print showing the true form of a working Bulldog.

how difficult it was before the age of mechanization to do certain tasks, such as controlling cattle on their way to market. Should a bull break away from its keeper, there was no jeep to head it off, and since medieval farmers could rarely afford a horse, there were no "cowboys" in the modern sense. The only solution was a strong, agile Bulldog which could be sent after the bull and trusted to have the courage, strength and speed to outrun it, grasp it by its sensitive nose and hold it until the men arrived. Because of its history as a "gripping" dog for ancient hunters, the Bulldog was uniquely suited for this work. He was in essence doing the same work, but now he held the animal for the butcher instead of the hunter.

There is a popular story that the sport of bullbaiting began with the witnessing of some Bulldogs at work by a nobleman who so enjoyed the spectacle that he gave the field where the animals were working to the townspeople to use each year on St. Bryce's Day for a baiting. In reality people had stood around and watched Bulldogs working for hundreds of years before this story took place, and indeed, the baiting of animals had been common in Roman times. It was inevitable that butchers would develop a contest to see which of their dogs was the most skilled at its work.

Because of this work, the Pit

A print from the personal photos of the Jessup family. This picture, taken in the early 1900s, shows a pioneer Pit Bull.

An old print showing a Pit Bull waiting for dinner after a hard day's work.

Bull to this day has a strong and natural tendency to grasp the nose of an opponent, and when working cattle it is almost impossible to get one to "heel" or stay behind and nip at the heels of the cattle. The Bulldog has a strong inbred desire to conquer the bull, not just to move it along as a herding dog would do.

In Fred Gibson's well-loved novel of *Old Yeller*, the dog controls unruly cattle by running alongside of them, gripping them by the nose and flipping them, a trait rarely seen in any but dogs of the Bulldog blood. It is safe to assume that Old Yeller, like many other pioneer dogs, was of Bulldog blood. Today there is little use for a true Bulldog, with jeeps and equipment for handling cattle. The dogs used today, like the Australian Cattle Dog and the Kelpie, are small, quick, nippy dogs, which move the cattle by nipping at their heels rather than stopping and holding them. With proper training, though, the Pit Bull can be trained to work cattle, though his style will be unique, and he may deal with a challenging bull with excessive force by today's stock-dog standards.

In the book *Cattle and Men*, the story of a bulldog crossbreed named Riley is told. The dog was given to a cowboy by the name of Jesse James Benton, who lived near Tombstone. When told to get a particular cow, Riley would catch the unbranded one by the ear or nose and hold it until his owner rode up. Then together the dog and man would down the cow in preparation for branding.

Another story from the Wild West tells of a large Pit Bulldog who was a favored house pet. He still wanted to work cattle though, and one day when the cattle got into the corn patch, he took purchase on the nose of a large steer. The steer was reported to be "swinging him around like a professional club swinger." By the time the dog was persuaded to release the steer, a considerable amount of corn had been flattened!

Another interesting account of a frontier Bulldog is mentioned in the publication *Outing* from 1887. The article is entitled "Bulldog versus Buffalo." It tells the story of a large white Bulldog named King, a favorite among the soldiers due to his size, strength and ferocity. He had been trained to pull down cattle at the slaughter yards of Fort Concho, and put this training to good use one day. A herd of buffalo was stampeding through the ranks of marching soldiers. King singled out the immense wounded leader and fastened on his neck. The bull went to his knees, "but so great was his strength that he quickly arose

"Daisy Mae" in obedience training. The fast and agile Bulldog loves this kind of competitive sport.

and whirled the dog in great circles over his head. King had been taught to never let go. The entire command now watched with breathless attention the apparently unequal struggle, expecting every moment to see the dog crushed to death. Down went the bull on his knees, this time not from any weakness, but to gore the dog; rising, he would stamp his feet in his rage, then shaking him a while, he would resume swinging and snapping him like a whipcord through the air." The fight ended, with "the dog, which had commenced the fight pure white, now turned a spotted crimson from blood which flowed from the buffalo's wounds, and still his brute instincts, tenacious courage and training led him to hold on. Had he let go for a moment, the crazed bull would have gored him to death before he could have retreated."

One can find stories of frontier Bulldogs being used to tackle all kinds of prey. R.B. Townshend mentions using a brindle Bulldog named "Keno" to hunt grizzly bears. "Sportsman" John Mortimer Murphy used Bulldogs crossed with Greyhounds to hunt wolves, some of which weighed in at 150 pounds.

As the Bulldog's use as a cattle-control dog came to an end, men turned the breed's strength and courage to other purposes. From man's fascination with violent encounters among animals came baiting sports, which pitted the dogs against a variety of animals. Written reports indicate that sending Bulldogs against lions, wolves, monkeys and even men was for a time a popular attraction. As human nature matured, tolerance decreased for these bloody, cruel and

Turn-of-the-century postcard showing a patient Pit Bull hooked to cart of lazy dogs.

"Sarona Trouble," a red/red-nose Pit Bull owned by Sarona Kennels in Wyoming.

Harry Clark and "Kager," a dog who won fights for several owners. This is an example of the large strain of Pit Bull from which the American Bulldog derived.

"Fighting Pit Bull" as their mascot. The popular sports team name "Bulldogs" comes from this era. "Tige," the Pit Bulldog companion of Buster Brown, as well as "Pete the Pup" of *Our Gang* fame also helped to boost the popularity of this breed. A female black brindle Pit Bulldog accompanied the explorer Stanley on his treks across Africa. He even mentions how the dog would bring down zebras by grasping them by the nose.

The early part of the 20th century was a time of explorers, new frontiers, and a bold, young, brave new era. The Pit Bulldog fit in well, hardy enough to accompany man anywhere he chose to go, good-natured enough to roam the streets with young boys. But times were

Above: A hard-working Bulldog bred by Bert Sorrels and owned by Stan Hiller. *Below:* York's Amber, a UKC-registered Pit Bull.

changing, and so was the working Bulldog. The world became more urban, more crowded, more "sophisticated." Successful businessmen no longer wanted a dog that was just a good-natured sidekick for their children, they wanted a status symbol, and the "purebred" dog was just becoming available to the common man. Instead of a rough and tumble companion, the trend was toward "elegant" and "foreign" breeds such as setters, Boxers and Dobermans. To make matters worse, with fewer Bulldogs being used as all-purpose companions, the breed was sustained primarily by fighters, with resulting changes in temperament. Whereas the Bulldog had always been a

Once again, the Bulldog is being bred to be the stable, adaptable, intelligent dog it has been through history. Owner, Ginny York.

commonsense type of animal, bred to be an all-purpose dog, stable, adaptable, and intelligent, suddenly a larger than usual portion of its population were being bred for "fighting drive" at the expense of common sense. This new development resulted in lines of fighting dogs which were hyper, nervous and uncontrollable around other animals. These lines are primarily found within registries which cater to dog fighters and the dogs are usually very small in size, often not even recognizable as purebred Bulldogs. The cruelest cut of all was the fact that the general public forgot just what a Bulldog was, and began thinking that the miserably malformed and useless show Bulldog registered with the AKC was the original Bulldog! All the positive qualities attributed to the working Bulldog were now given over to a non-working, non-functioning newly created show breed, and the real working Bulldog was to

Above: Ch. Red Kelly, owned by Dennis and Zuni Saccher, and Gr. Ch. Hansen's Jo-Mite, U-CDX, BH, WH, CGC, owned by Leri Hansen. *Below:* York's Silver Cloud, an AKC- and UKC-registered dog owned by John Froome.

become associated only with dog fighting. This was indeed unfair and untrue.

The 1980s saw the American Pit Bull Terrier gain again in popularity, but unfortunately this time as a "fad" breed, and as a result of a wide interest in dog fighting by street punks and drug dealers. Due to the actions of a few badly bred dogs in the hands of very irresponsible owners, the entire Bulldog breed suffered bad press. The very name "Pit Bull" came to mean something or someone vicious and aggressive. There have been laws passed banning all dogs which even resemble a Bulldog from certain communities, based on the action of one careless owner.

The challenge to tomorrow's breeders is to produce Bulldogs which again conform in appearance, temperament and ability to the original Bulldog of yesteryear. Each breeder must see himself as a steward of this ancient and wondrous breed, and see to it that each dog he produces is a true representative of all the qualities which make the Pit Bulldog what it is—the world's most versatile working dog.

This Pit Bull is dragging a tire behind him in training for weight pulling competition.

PR Ewing's Morgan, CD, TDI, U-CD, owned by Teresa Ewing.

Greenridge's Sarona Deadly Demon owned by Sarona Kennels. This Pit Bull shows almost perfect working-dog conformation.

THE UNITED KENNEL CLUB

In 1898 C.Z. Bennett set up a stud book for the Bulldog, and called it the United Kennel Club (UKC). He decided upon the official name of "American Pit Bull Terrier." The UKC had a knack for adding "American" to the front of just about every breed they registered and that explains why a very British (and Irish) breed became known as

"American." Also, the name "Pit Bull Terrier" was but one of a dozen the breed was known by, and was a rather unfortunate choice as it confused the breed with the real bull-and-terrier cross, the Bull Terrier. The reason that name was probably chosen was that it allowed the APBT to ride along on the then-tremendous popularity of the show Bull Terrier. Whatever the reason, because the name American Pit Bull Terrier was a rather inaccurate description of the dog, there remains a dozen other names the breed goes by, unlike other breeds which have a name that is undeniably correct (such as "Beagle" or "Rottweiler").

Above: Handsome and athletic Sarona-bred dog showing good Pit Bull conformation.
Below: York's Pudgie, a dog which shows good Bulldog form—strong, but still active.

Up until the UKC opened an official stud book for the breed, the dogs were known to their fanciers as Bulldogs, Pit Bulldogs, Pit Bulls and a few other names. It is eerie indeed when taking a modern APBT into a convalescent center to have the older residents point at the breeding plans secret. The UKC also offered standardized rules for dog fighting, and the sanctioning of official referees. The early UKC even offered the title of "Pit Champion" to any dog which had won three or more official fights. But the UKC was struggling to survive

AKC Ch. Rowdytown Piece of the Rock owned by Keith and Charlene Monske.

dog and say "Oh, a Bulldog like we had when I was a child!"

Bennett's idea was to allow Bulldog breeders to register their dogs under a central registry. He knew that meticulous records were kept on the breeding of the dogs, but that many breeders shunned registries for either monetary reasons or because they wished to keep their as a registry for APBTs only. Too many breeders still wanted to keep their pedigrees secret, and so the UKC opened its registries to the hunting hounds such as the Redbone, Bluetick and others. These breeders welcomed a "working dog" registry and hurried to register their dogs. The only other alternative at this time was the American Kennel Club which was interested only in dogs bred for appearance.

When Bennett died in 1936 the registry was taken over by his daughter and son-in-law. Through the years the UKC began to change as the acceptance of dog fighting as a "sport" declined. From its beginnings as a dog fighting journal, the UKC *Bloodlines* magazine has showcased the registry's changing attitude over the years. Ads which hint in any form about dog fighting are refused, and ads for dog-fighting equipment are also refused. Today the UKC maintains it will bar for life any person found guilty of dog fighting.

The UKC offers obedience classes for all purebreds and conformation shows for a growing number of breeds. There is a kind of race between the AKC and the UKC to see which registry will "snap up" each new breed. The AKC has even taken to accepting breeds against the wishes of some breed clubs! The UKC offers a variety of titles and services to hunting hounds. The emphasis of the UKC, as far as the APBT is concerned, is quickly becoming more and more "show" -oriented, while paying lip service to the "working" dog. Hopefully, in the future, the UKC, in keeping with its tradition of offering a service to the working dog breeder, will make changes necessary for the preservation of the breed as a functional working dog and not just another show dog. These

Ch. York's Ruffian Ashley, TT, a UKC- and AKC-registered female.

would include a mandatory OFA (hip dysplasia check) on the sire and dam of all litters being registered, and a requirement of at least a minimum working title on all dogs to be called "Champion." Since an OFA cannot be done before the dogs are two years of age, this would also stop the reckless practice of "finishing" (declaring a dog a champion) before the dog is two years of age. Like the AKC, the UKC could also go a long way toward improving the breed lobbying against irresponsible breeders, which would help to

Gr. Ch. U-CD York's Blue Bandit, TT, an American Staffordshire with cropped ears.

stop the tragic destruction of thousands of surplus Pit Bulls in animal shelters every year.

Official UKC APBT Standard for Conformation
(revised January 1, 1978)

HEAD: Medium length. Bricklike in shape. Skull flat and widest at the ears, with prominent cheeks free from wrinkles.

MUZZLE: Square, wide and deep. Well pronounced jaws, displaying strength. Upper teeth should meet tightly over lower teeth, outside in front.

EARS: Cropped or uncropped (not important). Should be set high on head, and be free from any wrinkles.

EYES: Round. Should be set far apart, low down on the skull. Any color acceptable.

NOSE: Wide open nostrils. Any color acceptable.

NECK: Muscular. Slightly arched. Tapering from shoulder to head. Free from loose skin.

SHOULDERS: Strong and muscular, with wide sloping shoulder blades.

BACK: Short and strong. Slightly sloping from withers to rump. Slightly arched at loins, which should be slightly tucked.

CHEST: Deep, but not too broad, with wide sprung ribs.

RIBS: Close. Well sprung, with deep back ribs.

TAIL: Short in comparison to size. Set low and tapering to a fine point. Not carried over back. Bobbed tail not acceptable.

LEGS: Large, round boned, with straight, upright pasterns,

A 40-pound brindle bitch with natural ears.

Head study of Gr. Ch. Dynamite Clone. Notice the flat skull and muscular neck characteristic of the breed.

reasonably strong. Feet to be of medium size. Gait should be light and springy. No rolling or pacing.

THIGH: Long with muscles well developed. Hocks down and straight.

COAT: Glossy. Short and stiff to the touch.

COLOR: Any color or markings permissible.

WEIGHT: Not important. Females preferred from 30-50 pounds. Males from 35-60 pounds.

SCALE OF POINTS

General appearance, personality and obedience	20
Head, muzzle, eyes, ears	25
Neck, shoulders and chest	15
Body	15
Legs and feet	15
Tail, coat and color	10
Total	100

UKC APBT Conformation Show Classes
(revised January 1, 1990)
PUPPY CLASS—Male: For all males six months to under one year. Winner receives ten UKC points.
JUNIOR CLASS—Male: For all males one year and under two years of age. Winner receives ten UKC points.
SENIOR CLASS—Male: For all

Winner receives ten UKC points.
(These same classes are then offered for females.)
BEST MALE OF SHOW is composed of winners of Puppy class, Junior class, Senior class and Veterans class. Winner receives 15 UKC points.
BEST FEMALE OF SHOW is composed of winners of Puppy

A UKC Champion bitch of Pit Bull and American Staffordshire blood, owned by Pam Wofford.

males two years and under three years of age. Winner receives ten UKC points.
VETERANS CLASS— Male: for all males three years and over.

class, Junior class, Senior class and Veterans class. Winner receives 15 UKC points.
BEST OF SHOW is composed of

Best Female of Show and Best Male of Show. Winner receives ten UKC points. (Total number of points possible to win at one show is 35.)

CHAMPION OF CHAMPIONS CLASS will consists of UKC-recognized male and female Champions competing against each other in the same ring at the same time.

GRAND CHAMPION CLASS is only open to those dogs that have earned their Grand Champion title (having won the Champion of Champions class three times under three separate judges). As these dogs have competed the highest conformation title awarded, no Championship points will be awarded.

NATIONAL GRAND CHAMPION CLASS is offered only at the fall National show, and will be made up of male and female

York's Just Peachy, registered with both the AKC and UKC, has earned 30 points towards championship status.

Pit Bulls compete in a number of specific classes in UKC competition. Owner, Joyce Klahn.

Champions competing against each other. The dog that wins this class will be the "National Grand Champion" for that year.

THE AMERICAN KENNEL CLUB
Thirty-eight years after the UKC started registering the Pit Bull, the AKC was petitioned by a few breeders who wished to register their dogs with the AKC to escape the unavoidable association with dog fighting that the UKC had at that time. The AKC made the decision to open its stud books to UKC-registered Pit Bulldogs for a time, but opted to change the name of the breed to remove the

Above: *Gr. Ch. U-CD York's Blue Bandit, TT.*

Below: *Spartagus, owned by Cindy Herron, won the first Champion of Champions Class at the UKC Nationals in Las Vegas, Nevada.*

AKC/UKC Gr. Ch. Estrella's Jac of Diamonds, registered as an American Staffordshire Terrier and as an APBT. Bred by Estrella Kennels.

word "Pit." In 1936 the AKC recognized the Pit Bulldog as the "Staffordshire Terrier," and one of the first dogs to be "dual registered" as both an APBT and as a Staffordshire Terrier was Pete the Pup of *Our Gang* comedy fame. Since that time there have always been certain lines of Pit Bulls which have been dual registered (meaning registered with both the AKC and the UKC). The AKC opened its stud books to the UKC-registered dogs again in 1972, and then closed them for good. UKC dogs are no longer allowed to be registered with the AKC. The UKC, on the other hand, still allows AKC dogs to be registered as UKC APBTs.

To add to the confusion, the AKC originally started registering the Pit Bull as the "Staffordshire

A blue brindle UKC-registered dog with AKC lines in its pedigree.

Terrier." They then changed the name to "American Staffordshire Terrier" when they recognized the "Staffordshire Bull Terrier" from England. At this point there were three different names for the same breed that had diverged slightly into three different lines of the same breed or type. The three breeds, APBT, American Staffordshire Terrier and Staffordshire Bull Terrier were all of the same blood—nothing had been added to make one a substantially different breed from the other. As if that wasn't bad enough, AKC Am. Staff breeders, and even the AKC itself began stating that the UKC dogs were not related to the AKC dogs developed from those same dogs! During the 1980s' "fad panic" concerning "Pit Bulls," the AKC even went so far as to state that there was no such breed as the Pit Bull because it was not recognized by the AKC! It should be noted that of the roughly 400 dog breeds in the world today, only about 130 are recognized by the AKC.

What the AKC wanted, it has created. American Staffordshire is considered by many a name more respectable than Pit Bull, and the dogs are bred for conformation show points. There are many good working Am. Staff lines, but this must be considered in spite of, rather than because of, AKC influence. AKC dogs do tend to have a much higher incidence of hip dysplasia, and some lines are plagued with shyness, but in all honesty these same faults can be found in dogs from all registries.

Official AKC Standard for the American Staffordshire Terrier:

GENERAL IMPRESSION: The American Staffordshire Terrier should give the impression of great strength for his size, a well put-together dog, muscular, but agile and graceful, keenly alive to his surroundings. He should be stocky, not long legged or racy in outline. His courage is proverbial.

HEAD: Medium length, deep through, broad skull, very pronounced cheek muscles, distinct stop; and ears are set high. **Ears**—cropped or uncropped, the latter preferred. Uncropped ears should be short and held half rose or prick. Full drop to be

At right: Ch. York's Tiffany, TT owned by Ginny York. **Below:** AKC Rowdytown Piece of the Rock owned by Keith and Marlene Monske.

penalized. **Eyes**—Dark and round, low down in skull and set far apart. No pink eyelids. **Muzzle**—Medium length, rounded on upper side to fall away abruptly below eyes. Jaws well defined. Underjaw to be strong and have biting power. Lips close and even, no looseness. Upper teeth to meet tightly outside lower teeth in front. Nose definitely black.

NECK: Heavy, slightly arched, tapering from shoulders to back of skull. No looseness of skin. Medium length.

BACK: Fairly short. Slightly sloping from withers to rump with gentle short slope at rump to base of tail. Loins slightly tucked.

SHOULDERS: Strong and muscular with blades wide and sloping.

BODY: Well-sprung ribs, deep in rear. All ribs close together. Forelegs set rather wide apart to permit chest development. Chest deep and broad.

TAIL: Short in comparison to size, low set, tapering to a fine point; not curled or held over back. Not docked.

LEGS: The front legs should be straight, large or round bones, pastern upright. No resemblance of bend in front. Hindquarters well-muscled, let

This dog is registered with the AKC and CKC as an American Staffordshire and with the UKC as an APBT. Can. Ch. White's Blue Light, owned by Ed LeBlanc.

TERRIER
GROUP 4TH
ARNPRIOR
CANINE
ASSOCIATION
14 MAY 89
W PRINTS PHOTO

AKC Ch. Mithrel's Red Outlaw, OFA, CD, showing cropped ears. Owner, Brenda Lilly.

dog fighting paraphernalia (including T-shirts with pictures of dogs fighting on it). The ADBA offers "conformation" shows in which the dogs are supposedly judged on their conformation, yet the dogs are presented lunging about on their leads. At one show the author recently attended, the winning dog was never even in clear view of the judge, as a ring of people stood around the dog to keep it from seeing the other dogs. The ADBA show is a parody of a real conformation show, and in some states their "weight pulls" bear no resemblance to real

Bonilla's Ms. Mar-grit from Dynamite Kennels.

York's Baby Blue, a UKC/AKC-registered dog owned by Debbie Morrison.

Gr. Ch. Hansen's Dynamite Boots.

weight pulls sanctioned by the International Weight Pull Association or other legitimate pulling organizations. ADBA weight pulls allow "baiting" of the dog with anything from a toy to the utterly tasteless use of small animal cages. There had been a recent trend toward presenting a better image on the part of the ADBA, and it can only be hoped that it will continue. In some parts of the United States, ADBA weight pulls are the only sanctioned pulls available, and many responsible weight pullers have had no choice but to attend them. These pullers are easily spotted as having well-mannered dogs which pull on command (without baiting). It is probably due in great part to the influence of these people that the recent changes to the ADBA have taken place.

Responsible breeders and owners of APBTs understand that the use of dogs to fight one another for sport has no practical or moral use in today's society. Dogs cannot be bred for, nor encouraged to, attack and kill animals to which they are going to be living in close proximity all their lives. The traits of gameness (desire to complete a task) and courage can still be bred for, but aggression toward other dogs has no practical application at all and is a detriment to the dog's use as a working or pet animal. While good dogs can be found among the members of any registry, responsible breeders tend to shun registries which condone dog fighting in any way.

Revolte's Jan, an American Staffordshire owned by Rudy Kasni.

The Bulldog Family Tree— Related Breeds

HISTORY OF THE PIT BULL AND RELATED BREEDS
ANCIENT HISTORY—"GRIPPING DOGS"

A specialized type of dog used with hound packs for closing in and gripping the animal until hunters could arrive to spear it. Described as shorthaired dogs of medium size with short, wide muzzles and proverbial courage.

MIDDLE AGES—"BANDOG" OR "BULLDOG"

The type is even more specialized now, and used almost exclusively as gripping dogs in hunting or as butcher's dogs for controlling cattle. Contests are developed to see which Bulldog is the best at his work and thus bull-baiting is developed. Bulldogs are sometimes

Gr. Ch. PR Whole Lotta Rosie, U-CDX, SchH III, CGC, OFA bred by Dennis Saccher and owned by Leri Hansen and Ch. PR Tobar's Shaka, CGC owned by Carlos Tobar.

called Bandogs, meaning "Tie-Dogs" for they are tied up when not working.

1800s—"BULLDOGS" AND "PIT BULLDOGS"

With the outlawing of bullbaiting, some Bulldogs are turned against each other in dogs fights. Most Bulldogs still work as butcher's dog, and many are going to America to become pioneer dogs.

1860—"BULL TERRIER"

James Hinks develops a strain of crossbred Pit Bull/White English Terrier dogs which he calls Bull Terriers. These dogs are all white and become very popular as show dogs and companions to sporting gentlemen.

1898—"AMERICAN PIT BULL TERRIER"

United Kennel Club is formed by C.Z. Bennett and begins registering Bulldogs as American Pit Bull Terriers. The name reflects Mrs. Bennett's desire to capitalize on the then-popular "Bull Terrier," as well as his attraction to the smaller fighting strains of APBT which did have some terrier in them. He also begins a tradition of renaming breeds with the word "American" before their name, even for breeds, like the Pit Bull,

"Diego," an American Staffordshire owned by Dan Schwarzle.

Gr. Ch. Lar-San San Krimson Chas Krug owned by Sandy Comer.

which were in no way American.

1910—"WHITE BULL TERRIER"
The White Bull Terrier is now fixed as a show breed. Some breeders begin to breed back to APBTs in an effort to improve temperament, and the result is the Colored Bull Terrier. These colored dogs are denied recognition as purebreds by most breeders and the AKC.

1935—"STAFFORDSHIRE BULL TERRIER"
The Staff Bull, the stay-at-home brother to the Pit Bull in America, is now recognized as a show breed in England.

1936—"COLORED BULL TERRIER"
Colored Bull Terriers are now accepted as purebred by the AKC after a long and heated debate as to their purity by the breeders of White Bull Terriers.

1936—"STAFFORDSHIRE TERRIER"
The AKC now opens its stud books to the UKC-registered APBT. "Pete the Pup" is now dual registered as an AKC Staffordshire Terrier and as a

UKC APBT. AKC changes the name to keep the word "pit" out.

1972—"AMERICAN STAFFORDSHIRE TERRIER"

The AKC changes the name of the breed when it realizes that the "Bulldogs" that stayed in England are called

changes in the two breeds' appearances.

PRESENT—"THE PIT BULLDOGS" Registered with the UKC as the APBT, with the AKC as the Am. Staff, and with the Kennel Club of England as the Staff Bull. Known to its breeders as "Pit Bull," "Pit

Sagebrush Tacoma Dreamer, TT, OFA owned by Carla Restivo.

Staffordshire Bull Terriers, and look slightly different than the American dogs. The AKC also opens its stud books to the UKC-registered dog again for a time.

1974—"STAFFORDSHIRE BULL TERRIER"

AKC recognizes the Staff Bull as a different and separate breed from its American counterpart. Time and distance have caused minor

Bulldog," "APBT," "Pit Bull Terrier," and of course, "Bulldog"!

Like the terms "coonhound" and "birddog," the name "bulldog" can also apply to the whole group of dogs which have descended from the original bulldog type. Of all the bulldog-type breeds, only the Pit Bull has remained a functional working dog. The rest have been developed into "show breeds,"

Lar-San's Oberon owned by Dennis Saccher.

with the resulting deteriorations of their character and soundness.

STAFFORDSHIRE BULL TERRIER
(AKA: Staff Bull, Staffy Bull, Staffordshire, Staff, Staff Bull Terrier)

The UKC opened its stud books to the Bulldog in 1898 and included dogs living in America. What became of the original Bulldog stock that stayed in England? Some Pit Bulldog lines were mixed with Pugs and other breeds and became the show breed known as the "Bulldog." Others were used for fighting and other baiting sports and bred down in size to better survive harsh economic conditions. These smaller dogs were developed into a show breed called the Staffordshire Bull Terrier, after the area in England where it was primarily bred.

The Staff Bull has been bred along slightly different conformation lines than the APBT or Am. Staff, being slightly smaller and generally broader. The ears are never cropped, and the dog is a very pleasing little animal, jolly and sweet-natured. In its native England the breed is considered the ideal child's dog; it is small in

The Staffordshire Bull Terrier is bred slightly smaller than its American counterpart. Photo by Isabelle Francais.

size yet sturdy and steady enough to take any abuse in good humor. The Staff Bull is generally good natured around other animals, but will, because of its heritage, soundly thrash any larger dog which challenges it.

BULL TERRIER
(AKA: Bullie, English Bull Terrier, Patton's Dog, Spuds Dog)

Here is the reason for so much confusion about breed names! This is the only true bulldog-terrier cross; it was developed by James Hinks. Hinks was interested in developing the older fighting dog type into a more refined show dog, yet he was interested in keeping the temperament strong. He crossed numerous breeds, most notably the Pit Bulldog, several types of terriers and the Dalmatian. The dog that was developed looked very much like a very refined, white Pit Bulldog. The ears were cropped until ear cropping was banned in England, at which time naturally erect ears were bred for. The new breed found much favor as a show dog and companion to gentlemen about town who liked to be seen with a sporty but sophisticated dog at their heels. The Bull Terrier went on to become the "respectable" show and pet dog, while the original Bulldog (Pit Bull) stayed in the hands of serious dog fighters, butchers and pioneers.

Bull Terriers have today, through selective breeding, developed an odd-shaped head that is very distinctive. The dogs are fun, happy, and sweet-

The Bull Terrier, the only true bulldog-terrier cross, is identified by its oddly shaped head and sweet disposition.

natured with people, but remain combative with other dogs, due in large part to the feisty terrier blood in their background. They make fine pets for anyone with a well-fenced yard and plenty of time to spend playing with and exercising the dog.

BULLDOG (AKC)
(AKA: Show Bulldog, English Bulldog)

Around 1860 a group of show fanciers got together and developed a standard for what they thought a bull-baiting dog should look like (bull-baiting was outlawed by that time). They wrote up this standard and began crossing the working Bulldog with other breeds such as the Pug, in an effort to develop the deformities of structure called for in their "standard of perfection." The result, after several decades, is the pitifully deformed and unnatural breed called "Bulldog"

even developed stories pertaining to how the recently developed deformities helped the Bulldog's ancestors in bull-baiting. It is said that the heavy wrinkles around the face allowed blood to drain away from the nose of the Bulldog as it clung to the bull, and that

The English show Bulldog, an AKC-registrable breed.

by the AKC. This breed, with its deformed nose, too-wide chest, short legs and too-large head is all but incapable of natural reproduction, and indeed cannot function normally in temperatures much above 70 degrees.

    Show Bulldog breeders have

the short, pushed-back nose allowed the Bulldog to breathe as it maintained a firm grip on the bull's nose. The fact is, dogs which fight each other for upwards of four hours in pits do not require such a deformed nose, and they maintain holds through

The Boston Terrier is a happy and brave little bulldog. Owner, Anna Benedetto. Photo by Isabelle Francais.

the duration of the fight. Also, no pictures of Bulldogs with such a shortened nose can be produced from any of the numerous etchings and drawings of bull-baitings from medieval times. The modern show Bulldog is incapable, due to structural faults, of any work, and is a testimony to the folly of breeding a dog to *look* like what a person *thinks* a working dog should look like!

BOSTON TERRIER
(AKA: Boston Bull, Boston Bull Terrier)

The Boston Terrier was developed around the Boston area near the turn of the century from small strains of Pit Bulls bred with terriers. The Boston is a definite bulldog type, happy and brave. They have always been popular as small, clean, quiet house and apartment companions, and are especially enjoyed by older people who do not wish to keep a larger dog which requires more exercise.

FRENCH BULLDOG
(AKA: Frenchie)

The Frenchie is another show version of the Bulldog type, bred in France but definitely of English Bulldog origins. The French bred the show Bulldog down in size, bred for an erect ear instead of a rose ear and concentrated on creating a smaller version of the show Bulldog. In all probability, a little Pug was probably bred in to help produce the shortened muzzle. A happy, sturdy dog, and a wonderful pet. Some health problems exist in this breed as a result of deformities called for in the show standard.

BULLMASTIFF

Developed in England by breeding Bulldogs with Mastiffs, this is a straightforward dog that combines the size of the Mastiff with the working ability of the Bulldog. A large, powerful dog, it is today bred only as a show and pet dog. It is one of the only two

Overly large "bat" ears are characteristic of the French Bulldog. Photo by Isabelle Francais.

The Bullmastiff is a huge dog with tremendous working ability. Owner, Debbie Jones. Photo by Isabelle Francais.

breeds (the other being the Doberman) bred *expressly* for the purpose of being used in defense work against humans. The purpose of the Bullmastiff was to apprehend poaching suspects without seriously injuring them. To this end he was taught to knock a person down yet refrain from biting, as a dog of such size and strength could too easily cause severe injures to a person in the event of an attack. Due to his being bred primarily for show points in the past few decades, the health and vigor of this breed is in serious question.

The Boxer is a variation of the Bulldog developed in Germany. Owner, Frederick Winkler. Photo by Isabelle Francais.

BOXER

The Boxer is yet another variation on the original Bulldog, but this one was developed in Germany. Early Boxers were almost indistinguishable from modern-day APBTs, and their temperament, too, is similar. The history of the Boxer in Germany is almost a mirror of the Pit Bull in England. First developed as a "gripping" dog for boar hunting, it was later used for a time as a dog fighter. It saw use during both World Wars as a police and war dog. Unfortunately for the Boxer, its flashy appearance and proud nature made it an ideal show dog, and soon a "standard of perfection" which called for a non-functional muzzle and jaw structure was developed. Rather quickly, the Boxer became just another show version of the Bulldog type. Without doubt he is very closely related to the Pit Bull, and comes from the same ancestors, simply developed in another country along slightly different lines. Robbed of a functional jaw though, the Boxer is seeing less action as a police, guard and sport dog. He still remains an outstanding pet who is intelligent, striking and friendly.

AMERICAN BULLDOG

A breed that until the late 1980s was virtually unheard of, this breed, I believe, was "manufactured" from existing lines of large pit bulldogs during the eighties to attract the novice Pit Bull owner who thought "bigger is better." Some lines are

A nice looking Pit Bull bitch lying next to an American Bulldog. Both owned by Tom Dubat.

probably pure Pit Bulls which survived and developed along unique lines in secluded Southern states. Some lines of this "purebred" are APBTs crossed with any of a half dozen large Mastiff-type breeds. This breed has been endowed with a rich and rather fictional history by the breed's promoters. These dogs are rarely fought, but instead are sold as a sort of "super guard dog" endowed with all sorts of supernatural abilities. It is marketed almost exclusively to those people who want a "big Pit Bull" for guard or attack work.

The breed has a fair-sized and loyal following, and are indeed handsome animals. A few people, particularly Al Banuelos of California, have had great success in Schutzhund with the dogs. Al Banuelos and his dogs are world-class competitors and have taken the top honors at many a high-level Schutzhund trial from traditional German breeds. Mr. Baneulos has stated that the smaller, more athletic Bulldogs work out best for sport or work.

The breed is going through a time of intense popularity and anyone interested in purchasing an American Bulldog would be well advised to require complete health exams of all breeding stock (including OFA exams) and would be advised to check into the temperament of the dogs as well. Though its breeders claim it is an ancient breed, the health

The American Bulldog is almost identical to the Pit Bulldog, and is identified by its massive size.

problems the breed is going though are characteristic of a newly created crossbreed, or a breed of dog developed from a too-small group of original breeding stock. A great many American Bulldogs are produced by kennels which breed several litters a year and increasing problems with health are being reported. Because the dogs are being bred for increased size, panosteitis (lameness) is reported as being a problem from which some pups never recover. Oversized animals (those over 100 pounds) suffer from shortness of breath and other breathing difficulties.

The American Bulldog is a fine-looking animal, large, and generally white with some color spots. Ears are rarely cropped, and very much resemble etchings of early bull-baiting dogs. It is hoped that the many severe health problems in this handsome new line of Bulldog can be worked out, as it is bound to find many enthusiasts among those who want a larger Bulldog-type dog.

This dog could pass for a 40-pound Pit Bull, but in reality is a 96-pound American Bulldog.

Ebony, by Striker out of Niki.

Preservation of "Game-bred" Animals

Perhaps no other topic is so often and so hotly debated among fanciers of the Pit Bulldog (and game fowl) than the "preservation" of the breed. Preservation means different things to different people, and it is a thorny question with no easy answer. Is a breed preserved if it only looks physically like its ancestors? Is a breed preserved if it changes appearance radically yet retains its original abilities? And is a breed preserved if it has been an all-purpose dog, bred for many tasks, and is now only bred for one narrow purpose?

There appears to be three main camps among Bulldog breeders. First there are the "conformation"

Gr. Ch. Tyee's Satin Magic, U-CD owned by Joyce Klahn of Tyee Kennels.

Gr. Ch. UKC/AKC Ch. Rowdytown Hardroc Cafe owned by Jerry and Gigi Rooney.

show people who feel the breed is best served by continuing to breed dogs which conform to a written physical standard. Some of the pitfalls of this method are: standards which change with the whim of each new generation of fanciers; no working basis on which to judge which conformation points are important to true working dogs; exaggeration of certain physical traits to the detriment of agility and function and the neglect of temperament, drive and character. A dog may be awarded a championship as early as six months of age—long before the dog's temperament has developed. Therefore in a conformation show the dog may be judged to be a "perfect specimen" yet mature to be a vicious or shy animal. The fact is the show ring and the resulting breeding practices associated with the show ring have made modern dogs useless caricatures of their ancestors.

The Cocker Spaniel can no longer hunt due to loss of drive and exaggerated coat length. The Great Dane is a sickly and weak remnant of the once proud boarhound. And of course, our own breed, the Bulldog, stands as perhaps the most extreme example of ruination of show breeding. The dog called "Bulldog" by the AKC, and bred only as a show dog for over 100 years, is barely capable of breathing and natural reproduction—a very far cry from the true working Bulldog which has survived today in the Pit Bulldog.

There can be no question that current practices of breeding to physical standard has been the ruination of purebred dogs. Instead of growing stronger, more vigorous and sounder, our purebreds have developed into weak and senseless animals which die at an increasingly younger age due to an alarming number of hereditary diseases. Crippled by hip and elbow dysplasia, suffering and dying from bloat and a dozen other diseases, our modern dogs offer a sad testimony to the breeder's "art." A mixed breed from the local animal shelter lives a longer, healthier life than our "well-bred" dog.

By very definition, breeding for conformation points means

The Pit Bull thankfully remains one of the few true working purebreds today. Pictured is "Rip," a red/red-nose Pit Bull working in Schutzhund and weight-pulling at nine months. Owned by Charlie Holland.

choosing those points over some other value. Few dogs have perfect conformation *and* perfect character. The Bulldog was never meant as a show breed—it goes against his entire history. It will be a sad day indeed when the Pit Bulldog is bred only for show ring points only to become another generic, dull show breed.

The second camp consists of the "dog-fight" fanciers. The majority of these people don't

Dan Guerra, proud owner of show winner Gr. Ch. PR Guerra's Beringer, BH, CGC, OFA, UCD, shown here going Best in Show at a UKC event.

Above: Dr. Rudy Kasni with Jan, a pup, and "Pete." **Below:** The Pit Bull is much more than just a fighting dog. This handsome non-fighter is from Sarona Kennels.

actually match dogs (the number of people who actually match dogs is extremely small, just like the number of Pit Bulldogs actually ever used for fighting is extremely small) and most are just people seduced by the romantic history of the breed, and feel that dog fighting is the only way to keep the breed alive.

Assuredly the Pit Bulldog excels at fighting—no other breed can stand before him—but is this what the Bulldog was created for? Does it represent the bulk of his work and reason for being through the ages? The answer is no. The Bulldog has existed for thousands of years, as just that—a bulldog. The function of this breed was to work with large animals, first the boar and stag, later domestic cattle. The Bulldog earned his keep, his name and his reputation *on cattle,* not other dogs. He was pitted against a *variety* of animals, in fact against anything, and his goal was not to kill, but to hold. It is only in the past 200 years that he was fought with any regularity against his own kind, and even then only in small numbers.

One fact that is constantly ignored by "pro-fighters" is simply that at any given time the number of Pit Bulldogs engaged or kept specifically for fighting other dogs was extremely low. During the heyday of fighting, the UKC registered only nine pit champions! This breed has never been bred exclusively for fighting other dogs. Not in the past, and not now.

The Bulldog has been historical and primarily an all-purpose work dog specializing in gripping and holding. He has found work with hunters as a holding dog, with stockmen as a catch dog, with pioneers and farmers as a watchdog and stock dog, and with sadistic gamblers as a fighter and baiter. Far more Pit Bulls have lived the life of farm dog, watchdog, hunting dog, stock dog and family companion than have ever entered a pit.

Undeniably the Pit Bull excels as a fighter—but he excels at many things. He often makes Huskies and Malamutes look sick as weight-pulling dogs, winning class after class at national weight pulls; does this

A Pit Bull competing in a sanctioned herding trial on cattle. This, along with controlling runaway cattle, was the original work of the APBT.

mean he was bred as a weight puller? No, it simply means he has the nature to excel at whatever he applies himself to. The Bulldog's courage, ability to ignore pain while working, and tenacious grip—all developed while working as a gripping dog—stand him in good stead when set against his own kind. But a dog which is so quarrelsome as to attack without provocation all other canines would hardly flourish in an age when dogs ran loose and were rarely restrained. "Jack," the brindle Pit Bull in Laura Ingalls Wilder's famous "Little House" books travelled across several

certain amount of substance. Sixty-pound Pit Bulls were pitted against lions, wolves and men. What good is a 24-pound rat killer as a Bulldog? The spirit may be there, but the flesh is not equal to the job. Dog fighters have tended to breed very small, thin dogs with excellent stamina, but not enough bulk to handle any job except the destruction of their own kind. This is a case of just too much specialization—and not preserving the breed.

"To try and to win" then is the essence of the breed. One test of the Bulldog from a few hundred years ago included the dog's gripping an object such as a rope and hoisting it into the air. Below the dog fireworks would be shot off, and a good Bulldog would maintain its grip despite this. Crazy? Yes, but it did showcase the determination of the breed—the quality by which our breed is judged.

The dog fighters do a great disservice to our breed. Some feel the fighter alone preserves the breed when in fact he alone spells disaster and destruction. Breeding dogs for a trait that makes them a danger and a threat to creatures with which it must coexist puts them at odds with survival as a species in this modern age. A dog can be tough, game and determined without showing overt aggression toward other dogs. As a matter of fact, the more confident the dog, the less threat display (growling, lunging) the dog will show. Extreme confidence is, in fact,

states under her father's wagon, and while he growled at other dogs her father's command was enough to hold him back. Jack was very fierce with strangers and wolves, and ended up having to be chained up as Indians began to visit the cabin on a regular basis.

To pick but one job the Bulldog has performed through his long history—that of fighting against his own kind for money—is as big a mistake as picking just one aspect of him—his conformation—to breed for. The essence of the Bulldog is to try and to win—no matter what the task. The Bulldog was expected to win against whatever he was asked to tackle—not just other dogs. This calls for a

Sundance Tacoma Whitepaws, bred by Carla Restivo, alertly guards her home.

Bulldog in the opinion of the author.

Dog fighting is not the answer for our breed. If animal baiting was still legal perhaps this would be the closest thing to a performance test to retain old type and function. But thankfully human nature (in most cases) has matured beyond the point of enjoying the spectacle of two animals harming each other.

Today there are still a few baiting practices which are legally allowed. In America bears and pigs still have dogs set on them. While it is undeniable that attacking a bear is a true test of a dog's courage, it is also a hideous cruel practice to both the dog and the bear. In one recent description of a bear hunt, the hunter described how the dog was slapped so hard by the bear that his head landed on one side of the bear and his intestines landed on the other. No normal dog lover would willingly submit his dog to this kind of treatment for "sport." Perhaps at one point in our history, when man faced danger side by side with his dog, spear in hand, such risks shared by man and dog could be justified. Men who would stand the charge of a bear or boar with only a spear or sword could perhaps qualify to ask their dogs to face that risk beside a woodland assassin who, like a coward, either dresses in camouflage or otherwise, hides himself away to snipe at the animals, or who stays at a safe distance while the dogs do the work. These people do not deserve to even work with such dogs.

So how can the breed be preserved, and is preservation of such a dog important? It is difficult to explain the importance of preservation to those who do not value it. It is a personal thing—a stewardship of living history which has been handed down to us, entrusted to us to preserve, cherish and pass on. For hundreds of years the Old English gamecock and the English Pit Bulldog have stood as living symbols of British pride in those around them. Who would not rather surround themselves with animals whose actions inspire admiration rather than some cringing, lowly animal who inspires instead the epithets such as "cowardly dog?"

The answer lies with the third group of fanciers, admittedly a small group for now. Those who struggle to preserve through legal, socially acceptable activities, and who understand that preservation means body, mind and soul.

Above: *Sarona Peacemaker works on the farm. The Pit Bull's strength and willing attitude make him an ideal all-around farm dog.*

Those who preserve the dog that *tries and wins at whatever* is asked of it are those who are preserving the breed.

These breeders strive for soundness in body by breeding only OFA (a hip-dysplasia screening) "good" or "excellent" dogs. They do not breed animals which are either too small or too large. They come to understand structure and how

Below: *Ch. PR Oliver's Dynamite Rudy, a very impressive weight-pulling dog, shows particularly nice head structure.*

A Colby-line dog, PR Tyee's Buster, owned by Joyce Klahn.

gait and angulation work to point out the sound working dog. They understand that many show champions are dysplastic, and that the show ring is no place to judge either soundness or working ability.

These breeders place foremost importance on character—that thing which makes a dog great or mediocre, a menace or a companion, courageous or cowardly. And character is that something about a breed that attracts the true fancier.

The performance breeder should never lose sight of the fact that in this modern age the majority of pups end up in pet homes, and must be able to perform as such. That in itself is a worthy goal—to produce sound, healthy, well-adjusted puppies which will delight their owners and earn the family's

trust and respect. But the Bulldog is not for every home and his reason for being is not just to be a pet. There are plenty of breeds already in existence with this job.

How then do we preserve our performance breed? How do we maintain his status of game, trying dog—the super dog that does his master's bidding no matter how tired or sore? The dog that will grip "to the death" whatever object shown? Having preserved the working Bulldog in body and character, now we must test for that something that makes a Bulldog a Bulldog. He is a rugged, tough breed, and to remain so he needs a rugged, tough test, yet humane to himself and other creatures. Is this test to be found in current dog sports such as herding, Schutzhund, weight pulling?

Schutzhund is a fine sport, one which the author enjoys titling dogs in. It tests a dog's willingness, the trainer's skills, and the dog's ability to perform protection tasks. It tests many facets of the dog to a certain degree. Yet Schutzhund was developed for and around sheepdogs (like the German Shepherd), and remains a test best suited for their submissive, compliant and softer character. Schutzhund may test these breeds severely, but it remains somehow incomplete for the Bulldog. He can too easily fulfill these tasks of obedience, tracking and holding a man.

Schutzhund does remain the single best test of a Bulldog's

ability to work in our modern society. He must mingle with other dogs, listen carefully to his owner, perform socially acceptable functions such as tracking and protecting his owner. Done *well* it is an excellent accomplishment for a Bulldog, but far too many weak-nerved dogs are allowed to pass. A dog can get chased from the field by one agitator, then try again under another, weaker agitator and pass. Schutzhund is like any test—it must be honestly evaluated by the dog's owner, after a long, careful look at his own dog's temperament. Right now weak nerves are not a huge problem in our breed—but we must be vigilant to keep it so.

Herding as done today is only a test of a Bulldog's inborn herding

Above: *A vacationing Pit Bull does some California dreamin' in the hot sun.* **Below:** *Grand Ch. PR Tyee's Boy Bosworth, owned by Joyce Klahn.*

Spartagus proves his stability and training by doing the "hold and bark" of a suspect.

drive and willingness to try and please its owner. Herding trials today are based on sheepdog work and require that the animal stay away from the stock. This is in direct contradiction to the nature of the Bulldog, and while he certainly can and does work stock very well, this is no longer the game for him. Stockdog trials which would really test a Bulldog would be impractical in today's world. Herding will continue to be an indicator of a Bulldog's inborn ability to control stock, but great care must be taken to never put him against stock which will challenge his authority unless you can appreciate the full consequences of his reply. A Pit Bulldog will not let a challenge go unanswered.

Weight pulling is, perhaps, the closest "'parallel" to dog fighting available to those who feel the need for a closeness. Dogs are conditioned just like a fighter in a "keep" and fed and weighed carefully. The perfect pulling weight is like the perfect fighting weight, lean without being skinny, but at the lowest working weight. Dogs of similar weight are matched against each other, and may the best Bulldog win!

Weight pulling, though originally designed around

northern breeds, has adapted itself well to our breed. Because the classes are divided by weight no one has a tendency to breed oversized dogs. Agility might suffer, but the intelligent breeder will breed for more than weight pulling. Weight pulling is though, a tough test and well suited to our breed, and is for the most part humane. There will always be a few people who become so competitive they lose sight of common sense and decency and over-pull their dogs, but hopefully peer pressure to be more sportsmanlike will help to keep this in check. Those who must resort to fear tactics such as shocking sticks will soon realize that if you need to train with

Above: Bandog Bad working in a seminar.
Below: Bandog Dread bringing down his man in a Schutzhund exercise.

Above: A good solid pull at the IWPA 1994 championship. This dog shows excellent calm form, pulling with head down. IWPA pulls do not allow "baiting" the dog.

Below: 1994 IWPA championships. A 94-pound APBT was first in the 80-100 pound class. Photo by Carla Restivo.

Above: A beautiful bitch owned by Robert Phipps of San Diego. Excellent form and a well-padded harness. *Below:* Bulldogs ruled at the 1994 IWPA championships. Between pure Pit Bulldogs and American Bulldogs, almost all the top placements were captured. Here Mark Lander's American Bulldog shows a game effort to win second place in the 80-100 pound class. Photo by Carla Restivo.

fear you are training a sub-standard Bulldog anyway. A game dog needs no fear tactics to make him try his best.

To the author there is something uniquely Bulldog about the springpole. After all, ours is a breed renowned for its grip. More should be done to encourage competition with the springpole, as it is not only extremely enjoyable for the dogs, it is also something which is difficult to train with force. For those who prefer a smaller dog, a springpole is definitely easier for small dogs. Big, heavy dogs have a harder time maintaining an "air" grip for long periods.

Springpole does effectively test determination. The dog fights the rope (in his mind anyway) and the longer he maintains the fight, the gamer he is (game meaning willing to try whatever he is set at). Springpole also is a very effective measurement of

Above: B.W. Lightsey's Puller practices for his Schutzhund title. *Below:* An APBT bitch shows classic pulling style while taking first place at 1993 IWPA Pull-Off. Owner, Dean Tibbetts.

Dread and Brittania show great springpole form.

prey drive. In its way springpole (when the dog is airborne) measures structure also (can the dog hang on as long as it should?), heart or gameness (how long will they maintain their grip when bid to hold by their owner?), fighting drive (how long will the dog keep up its "fight" of the rope?) and obedience (will the dog release its hold on command?).

Preserving our breed lies with those who continue to do what those before us have done—ask many tasks of the dog and breed from dogs who try and win. The breeder and owner of a multi-titled dog has much to be proud of, for this is the Bulldog's future. He is the ultimate working dog just because he is the ultimate athlete. This is a breed that should be bred for a variety of purposes, but always for heart, strength, grip and courage. This is his heritage, and this is his future.

Left: Puller, a certified Search and Rescue dog, dares the suspect to try and escape. *Right:* Gr. Ch. Guerra's Beringer, U-CD, B, CGC, working the springpole.

Since the bull and terrier breeds are naturally aggressive towards other dogs, even play fighting between two housemates requires close supervision and should not be encouraged.

Dog Fighting Today

Depending on whom you listen to, there are two completely different realities of dog fighting. According to those who enjoy watching dogs fight, it is a sport enjoyed by hardworking good citizens who simply enjoy watching animals doing what they were bred to do. Of course it is difficult to prove these claims as dog fights are held in secret and most people do not claim to be dog fighters of their own free will.

The reality of law enforcement involvement with dog fighting is quite a different picture. Almost every bust involves seizures of

There are many different activities besides fighting that test the gameness of the Pit Bulldog.

large amounts of drugs, illegal guns and money. In fact, many dog-fight busts come about because of intelligence gathered during drug enforcement investigations. A bust which took place in Arkansas in 1979 netted the largest cache of illegal weapons and drugs ever seized in that state. The sum of

in the world of "professional" fighters, the dogs are generally found in a severely neglected state. As one example, the dogs seized in raids at 17 locations in Wayne and Washtenaw Counties, Michigan, were discovered in an emaciated, dehydrated and diseased condition. Dogs taken during a

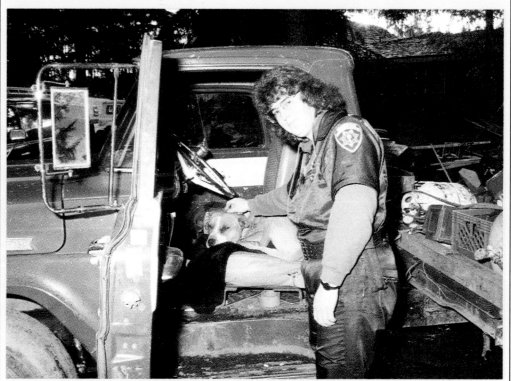

The author with a Pit Bull which was found during a drug raid. Swat teams requested that she remove this old and neglected dog from the truck it was living in.

$500,000 was found on the participants, and $7,000 in "gate" money was seized. along with 50 handguns, knives, cocaine, marijuana and hashish.

Proponents of dog fighting also paint a picture of superbly conditioned fighting dogs in the pink of health. The reality is something quite different. Even

raid conducted near Hepzibah, Georgia were found to be suffering from severe mange.

What attraction does dog fighting hold for its spectators? It is hard for those who enjoy their dogs as companions and friends to understand how anyone could enjoy watching dogs maul and seriously injure each other. Harder still to imagine cheering every broken limb, every chewed nose, every injured eye. The more severe the injury a favorite dog inflicts on its opponent, the louder the cheering and greater the joy of the spectators. While the dogs may indeed appear to be enjoying their battle, they certainly do not appear to be "happy warriors" in the days after the fight when many die of shock, injuries and infection. Dogs die of suffocation when their faces and nasal tissues swell from severe damage and they cannot breathe. Still others die of dehydration due to their being "dried out" before a fight by their owners, in the mistaken belief that a dehydrated dog will lose less blood and therefore be able to fight longer. It is not uncommon for a dog to lose three or four pounds just during the course of a fight— and that kind of stress can kill even without a fatal injury.

Prior to 1975, dog fighting was a misdemeanor in all 50 states. Since then the majority of states have passed felony laws; sometimes just for owning a dog with intent to fight. Intent is a very difficult thing to prove and in some cases law-enforcement officers have harassed innocent people who happened to resemble the sterotypical appearance of a dog fighter.

Intent may be inferred by ownership of Pit Bulldogs, a treadmill, springpole, breaking sticks, and magazines that emphasize dog fighting. Of course none of these things proves intent; in fact, ownership of a treadmill is common among breeders of different dog breeds to condition dogs for shows and field sports.

Some of the more obvious signs that a person is involved in dog fighting is a scarring of any dogs on the premises. Most dog breeds fight in a very haphazard fashion, slashing anywhere on their opponents' bodies. Most commonly dogs from non-fighting breeds will exhibit scars in a random pattern on their bodies. Due to selective breeding, most Pit Bulls will grasp an opponent either around the head/nose area or by the

An athletic and feisty young bulldog.

front legs. Pit Bulls which have fought other Pit Bulls will usually exhibit scars in these areas. Of course, any Pit Bull breeder or owner could have a dog which at one time got into a scrap and received a few scars in these areas, but any owner who owns multiple dogs with heavy scarring in these areas should be considered suspect.

A typical "pro" dog fight is held in the evening, usually on a Friday or Saturday night. Only a very few people will actually know the location of the pit and spectators and even participants will be collected from meeting places (generally bars) and driven to the site. Food and drink are generally available at

Brittania after an accidental scuffle with another Pit Bull. Can you imagine what two bulldogs would look like after a "pro" fight?

the sight and time is spent before the first fight betting, drinking, visiting and using or dealing drugs.

Rules and traditions of dog fighting are very old and strictly adhered to in a "pro" fight. None of these precautions or traditions are followed in impromptu fights, which are by far the most common type. A coin is tossed and the winner can decide whether to have his dog washed first or pick his corner of the pit. Dogs are washed under the close supervision of the handler and judge, to clean them of any poisons or other substances which may have been applied to their coats. The dogs are then dried and carried to their corners. At the referee's instructions to "face the dogs" the dogs are turned toward each other. At the order to "Let go!" the dogs are released. Unlike in a street-dog fight between two "cur dogs" (breeds other than those bred for fighting), there is very little noise when Pit Bulldogs fight, the only sounds are those of the dogs struggling, tissue being torn or crushed, and the cheers of the crowd.

The dogs do not snap and snarl but rather grab hold, often in a preferred spot such as the nose or stifle, and shake. Such shaking can be encouraged by the handler who may have conditioned the dog to do it on command. The damage to the dogs can be devastating, and many dogs are injured beyond repair in 15 minutes or less. The

An APBT picked up by Animal Control. This dog had been fought and then dumped. It was suffering from severe injury and was eventually put to sleep.

dogs are allowed to fight uninterrupted until one "turns," or makes a move away from its opponent. At that time the dogs are "picked up," "out of holds" (grabbed up as soon as both dogs are free of holds) and taken to their corners. After 15 seconds the dogs are again "faced" and the dog that turned is released first. The dog must "scratch" or re-attack its opponent directly. If it fails to do so either because it no longer wishes to fight or because it is too badly injured to cross the pit, it is declared the loser and most likely will be shot on the spot to save the owner the embarrassment of keeping a loser. If the dog re-attacks its opponent, the fight goes on with the dogs being picked up at each

turn and alternately scratched to the other dog. For a pit dog there are only three ways out of a fight. He must kill or so injure his opponent that it cannot continue the fight, become thus injured himself (and probably not survive), or he must be killed in the pit. If he quits he will be destroyed or left to die. Dog fights, if uninterrupted, will last from ten minutes to over four hours in the case of evenly matched and conditioned dogs.

The reality of who dog fighters really are can only be driven home after actually seeing how these people treat their dogs. Dogs have been left to die of starvation by well-known fighters when law enforcement officers have moved in. A bitch with a shoulder broken in a fight

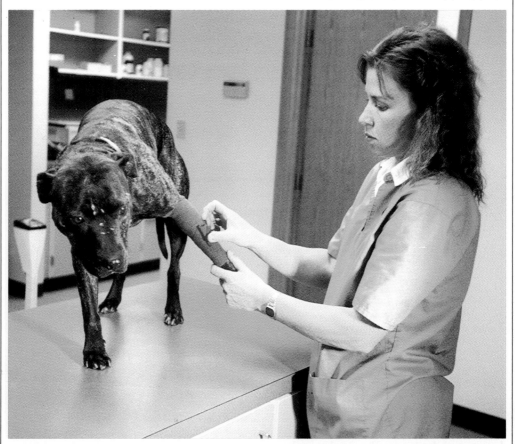

A Pit Bull getting wrapped up after an unintentional fight with another dog. And some people call dog fighting a sport?

and left unset was shipped to another fighter to be bred in that condition. These dogs spend their entire lives on heavy, short chains with very inadequate shelter. These owners are generally characterized by their inability to get along in modern society and by their disregard for law enforcement and society in general.

TERMS USED IN DOG FIGHTING

Ace: A winner of over five "professional" fights.

Breaking stick: A wedge-shaped stick used to break the hold of a fighting dog. It is not considered proper to use breaking sticks in an actual fight. They are commonly used during practice fights.

Bump: A practice fight for young dogs or dogs in training. Dogs are not conditioned for a bump, and are often left on their chain while fighting.

Catch weight: Any large dog over 52 pounds.

Cat mill: Rarely used, a conditioning device that consists of a central axle with two or more rotating arms radiating outward from the center. A lure is attached to one arm and a dog to another. The dog will chase the lure around in a circle, thus exercising himself.

Chain weight: Weight of a pet dog or any APBT not in fighting or working shape.

Champion: Winner of three professional fights.

Contract: A written agreement used during pro fights which specify: (1) date and time of fight, (2) weight of the dogs involved, (3) the referee, and (4) amount of the wager.

Convention: A major dog fighting event consisting of several matches. The ADBA, in keeping with its tradition of promoting dog fighting, calls its national conformation show a convention.

Courtesy scratch: After a fight, the losing dog is expected to show its desire to continue fighting in order for it to lose "right." Sometimes dogs are no longer able to walk at all and are expected to and applauded for attempting to push themselves across the pit toward the winning dog. The dog is not allowed to take hold and the winning dog is then allowed to scratch back. An entire section in one widely read APBT breed book was devoted to describing how moved the participants were at one fight when a severely injured dog struggled across the ring with broken legs and shoulders. The owner wept with joy.

Cur: Any dog other than an APBT, or an APBT that acts like a non-fighting dog (a coward).

Cur out: To quit or act like a coward.

Down dog: Dog on the bottom during a fight and usually receiving the worse punishment.

Facing off: Encouraging two APBTs to challenge each other by letting them get face to face and holding them there.

Fancier: Persons with an interest in dog fighting and the APBT.

Fanged: When a dog bites down through its own lip with a canine tooth.

Feed out: What a dog is fed.

Forfeit money: A certain amount of money that each dog fighter puts up front to be held

An APBT which ended up at an animal shelter and was destroyed after it was neither claimed nor adopted.

by a third party to assure that they will meet their obligations and produce a dog to be matched.

Gameness: The desire shown by a dog to continue the task at hand (in this case fighting), no matter how discouraged, tired or injured it may be. A dog may show its gameness in activities other than fighting, such as weight pulling or tracking. Gameness is not to be confused with dog aggression, which is the threat display of one dog toward another. The desire to start a fight has nothing to do with a dog's true depth of gameness.

Game Test: To fight a dog until he is so injured and tired that he can hardly stand and then see how he reacts when a fresh dog is pitted against him.

Grand Champion: A dog that has won five or more "official" fights.

Handle: To pick up and separate two fighting dogs. This is done after a dog turns (makes a move away from its oponent) in order to scratch the dog which turned (give it a chance to cross the pit and resume the fight) to see if it is game. Because a dog is not always handled by its own owner (the other dog's handler may be in a better position to pick the dog up when the dogs are out of holds) true fighting dogs are rarely aggressive to humans, even when excited by a fight.

In-breed: Breeding dogs which

This bulldog got into a scrap with her housemate. The veterinarian is checking for signs of swelling in the throat area, which would indicate infection.

are closely related such as father to daughter or brother to sister in order to "set a type" or temperament trait.

Keep: The conditioning of a dog, generally used by fighters and some weight pullers. The dog is intensely conditioned, dieted and trained for weeks before an event in order to peak the dog the day of the event.

Match: The dog fight.

Matchweight: The weight agreed upon by both owners that the dogs will weigh the day of the fight.

Mouth: When the fighting dogs are so tired and injured they can no longer bite with any power, they are said to mouth each other.

Pit: The area where the dogs fight. Only in a professional fight would an actual pit be used, which is constructed of plywood and usually 16 feet square and about 3 inches high. "Punk fights" are held in sand boxes, school grounds, cattle-loading chutes, empty swimming pools, etc.

Promoter: Person responsible for setting up the fight, its location, trophies, food and security. He receives the gate money.

Pumping up: Dogs are walked about and encouraged to be aggressive towards the other dog before the match to make sure they will fight when released in the pit.

Red/Red Nose: A coloration of APBTs in which the dog is a solid red color (from light tan to deep red) and the nose, nails and eye rims are pink or red.

A red/red-nose APBT with ears that have been cropped rather long.

Red/Red Noses are often called "Old Family Reds" because one line did come from Ireland and were called by that name. The actual "Old Family Red" line no longer exists in a pure state. Many novices consider the Red/Red Nose to have special abilities as a pit dog due to their strange appearance.

Referee: A third person in the pit that decides when a dog turns and other matters.

Ringing: Severely injuring tissue around another dog's leg in a circle by maintaining a bite on the leg but moving the grip around.

Roll: See *Bump.*

Rough mouth: A dog that

Tara Colby, a purebred Colby Pit Bull, owned by Sonja Buckley.

The Colby Family of Dogs

To discuss the Colby family, and the Colby family of dogs, is to discuss the history of the Pit Bulldog (as a fighting dog) from almost the beginning of organized fights in the United States until the present day. John P. Colby was born in America, however, he is forever linked with Ireland, as he imported a great many Irish immigrants, Irish fighting cocks, and Irish fighting Pit Bulldogs.

John owned his first Pit Bulldog in 1883, and bred his first litter in 1889. John's son, Louis Colby, still lives in his father's hometown of Newburyport, Massachusetts, and still maintains the same lines of fowl and Bulldogs which his father developed. The Colby dogs have not changed much in 100 years— they have not been subject to the fickle whim of the show ring. Their friendly, game,

Louis Colby, son of John Colby, at the Colby place in Newburyport, MA. Pictured with him is John Fonseca, who developed a line of dogs using Colby blood.

trustworthy temperaments have also come through the ages intact, and are perhaps the trademark of these dogs.

John Colby's first litter in 1889 was from straight Irish and English bloodlines. Though John, in the words of his son, "never worked five minutes for any man," he did, however, employ a great many men, and it was said that he would hire any

keeping on his animals. Many of his handwritten pedigrees survive to this day. A great many, if not most, modern American Pit Bull Terriers can trace their pedigrees back to a dog John Colby either imported or bred—such was his importance to the breed.

In 1936 the American Kennel Club formed a committee headed by Wilford T. Brandon to

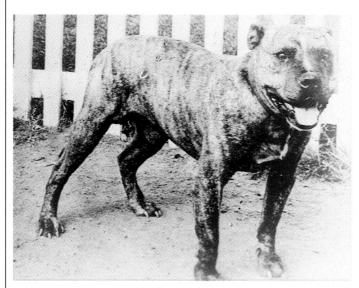

An old photo of Colby's Paddy, a dog which closely resembles the look of many current Colby dogs.

Irishman who would bring along a good dog or two from the homeland. John owned a strip of land that ran completely through the middle of a block in Newburyport. Because of this his property actually had three houses on it. Son Louis states that while the family lived in one house, the dogs and fowl lived in the other two! John bred and fought his Pit Bulldogs, and also was known for keeping a game strain of fowl, mostly Irish pyles and Irish roundheads. He had a reputation for scrupulous care in breeding, raising and record-

establish a standard for the appearance of the Pit Bulldog. The committee went about the county looking at Pit Bulls, and settled on Colby's Primo, owned by John Colby, as the closest to perfection on the basis of physical appearance. The AKC went ahead with drawing up the standard of the Pit Bull, using Primo's picture as the best type. They did, of course, change the breed name to "Staffordshire Terrier," but it was a UKC-registered Pit Bulldog which served as the model for the AKC standard.

Colby's Galtie, a beautiful modern Pit Bulldog that looks exactly like the Colby dogs of 100 years ago.

The Colby family registered their dogs with the AKC for about three years, as a courtesy gesture for their using Primo. However, they continued to register with the older UKC, with which they had been registering since the turn of the century, and gradually stopped registering their dogs with the AKC. Thus the Colby dogs returned to being "Pit Bulls" instead of "Am. Staffs."

It is interesting to note also that the first Staffordshire Terrier champion of Canada was a dog bred and sold to that country by the Colby family. This dog, Horner's Luger, was owned by Clyde Lovett, and was crowned champion on July 15, 1952.

John Colby is well represented in his son, Louis. Louis Colby is a true gentleman, who has what appears to be a photographic memory which encompasses dogs and chickens back for 100 years. He speaks of the birthdates of dogs dead 80 years as easily as a parent speaks of their own child's birthday. Louis grew up around his father's dogs and chickens, and indeed he can be seen in many of his father's photographs of the animals. He owned his first dog in 1932, when he was 11.

Louis Colby lives in Newburyport, on a beautiful farm (he is a dairy farmer) where his dogs and fowl are kept in splendid facilities. His dogs live in spacious kennel runs, each with a triple insulated dog house filled with clean straw, and with a flap over the door. Unlike so many people who keep multiple dogs, Louis Colby shows the care and attention to detail which keeps his animals healthy and very comfortable. Every dog on his farm is friendly and approachable, and he would have it no other way. He is truly of the "old school," the type you just don't find anymore. He is far removed from the type of people involved in fighting animals today.

When asked how the Colby family has maintained the type and gameness of their strain for so many generations, Louis stated the answer is "keeping as

Colby's Dolan, sire of a great many modern Colby Pit Bulls. Very typical Colby appearance.

many males as females." A common mistake in breeding, he asserts, is to keep several females but only a "main" stud dog or two. This, he says, leads to "breeding yourself into a corner in a few years." Even during the depression days his father maintained several stud dogs to keep the line strong. Louis Colby also states emphatically that the standard is 35-65 pounds, and he breeds to that. There are two kinds of Colby dogs you'll never see—red nosed reds and oversized. The Colby dogs are medium-sized brindles and fawns. The males tend to be much heavier in build than the females.

Colby's Galtie, circa 1940. In this dog it is possible to see the kind of dogs used around the Boston area to produce the Boston Terrier.

Though Louis Colby raises both dogs and fowl that have seen action in the pit for generations, he understands that "fighting dogs" appeal to a great many people who do not like dog fights. He recognizes that the vast majority of his dogs go into family homes, and he seems to have no qualms about that. He stated to the author, "You won't see many of my dogs in the pit—but when you do you'd be smart to put money on 'em."

Asked about the complex issue of "gameness," Louis had the following to say: "You can't make a poor one a good one. And they're not like game fowl where an entire hatch (litter) will be good. You have a much higher percentage of game in a hatch of fowl than you do in a litter of dogs." He also said that far too many good dogs are ruined by

owners who rush the dogs, and ask too much too soon. A dog that quits at 15 months may turn out to be a great dog at two years. When asked if a person could keep a line of dogs true to Bulldog virtue and strength and maintain gameness without fighting their dogs he replied, "Yes, I think so." He added that *dog aggression* had nothing to do with gameness and stated "they don't have to be aggressive to be game—they don't have to reach out and grab everything to be game."

Asked how to best determine gameness in a pup he stated it was impossible to tell in a pup. The best way to determine gameness in a mature dog is through work. "A dog that will quit in its work will quit in a fight; if he won't take his work then he

*Above: Colby's Bud. **Below:** Bandog Colby Jack, one-half Colby breeding.*

will lay down and quit in a fight." The work, he said could be many things, weight pulling being among one of the best choices.

Louis Colby doesn't advertise his dogs, and hasn't for some time, yet he receives two to three calls every evening from people who have sought him out. To own a pure Colby dog is to own a piece of history. It is an honor really, for no other line has been so carefully preserved. Dog lines come and go, but Colby's line, like the Pit Bull himself, perseveres and survives.

Above: This is a very rare photo of Galvain's Pup. He is the most famous fighting dog ever and ancestor of many Colby dogs. *Below:* Colby's Lotus.

PR Cheek's Red Baroness, SchH III, U-CDX.

Common Myths about Pit Bulls

All breeds have myths associated with them, but the Pit Bulldog may have more than its share due to its strength and abilities. This is compounded by the fact that few people actually know the breed well. Some myths are harmless—a wee bit of an exaggeration of the breed's abilities in weight pulling or as a guard dog, for instance. Others are very damaging, such as tales of unstable temperament, viciousness or "locking jaws."

Every breed which has had a brush with popularity collects

Most myths associated with the Pit Bull are very damaging to the breed. This is Bandog Sledgehammer U-CD, owned by Royal Kennels.

A beautiful head shot of AKC Ch. Misty Moonshine TT, owned by Keith and Charlene Monske.

myths which take on the status of "fact" with the general public. The Doberman, popular as a fad breed in the late '70s, had many, many negative myths created about it. Some of the most enduring myths recount how the dogs will turn on their owners, or that their brains are too large for their skulls, causing them to go crazy. While nothing could be further from the truth, it is still possible to find dog people, even some veterinarians, who will tell you this is true.

What has harmed the Pit Bull perhaps more than anything are the writings of self-proclaimed Pit Bull experts, which continue to put forward the myths that the breed is good only for fighting, is uncontrollable around other dogs, and should be kept only on a chain. While these authors show their ignorance in their every word, once published, the damage is done, as many novice owners trust any advice they get from a book. It is the unfortunate truth that in the case of many myths, the breeders and owners of the American Pit Bull Terrier are its own worst enemy.

Some common myths and misconceptions follow:

PIT BULLS ARE NOT A PURE BREED

There is no breed registered as simply "Pit Bull" with any registry. There are, though, at least two purebred dog registries that register "American Pit Bull Terriers," from which the shortened nickname "Pit Bull" is derived. Pit Bulls are indeed a very ancient and very pure breed of dog; some lines of Pit Bulls are considered to be of the purest breeding in dogdom, such as the Colby line which has been linebred by the same family since before 1900.

The American Kennel Club, because it registers Pit Bulls under the name of "American Staffordshire Terriers," and because it does not care to acknowledge the existence of its closest competitor, the United Kennel Club (which does register APBTs), has publicly stated that there is "no breed of the Pit Bull," because it is not registered by the AKC or the CKC (Canadian Kennel Club). The AKC continues to act as if the purebred Pit Bulldog (the same dog it welcomed into its stud books in 1936 and 1972) does not exist. Many more Pit Bulldogs are registered each year with the UKC than American Staffordshires are registered with the AKC.

Confusion occurs when attempts are made to label true mixed-breed dogs as "Pit Bulls," a very common occurrence on bite statistics, police reports, hospital reports and in newspaper accounts of dog bites. One large newspaper even misidentified a purebred Akita which had severely mauled a five-year-old as a "Japanese Pit Bull." The Akita is a large spitz (husky) type dog and in no way resembles or is related to the Bulldog family.

In one West coast city a police officer was bitten while standing in the street watching an animal-control officer attempt to subdue an aggressive German Shepherd. The dog, described by witnesses as a "large, white,

Both the UKC and the ADBA recognize the American Pit Bull Terrier as a purebred. This is Castillo's Savoy Brown.

Ebony, a UKC Champion owned by Teresa and Peter Beach.

develop a strong resemblance to the standard by which the breed is judged. Appearance, in other words, is the performance by which the dogs are judged and bred for.

In true performance dogs, a breeder looks at the ability and soundness of a dog, and then breeds it to a dog with the same abilities and soundness— regardless of appearance. Because of this you have APBTs that weigh 28 pounds, and APBTs that weigh 90 pounds. That is also why some strains are very thin and racy and others are wide and broad, and why they are all colors and builds. And this is also why it is almost impossible to describe a Pit Bull or to define what one looks like.

Another factor to be considered is that dog fighters don't care at all if their dogs are purebred, they care only that they win. While dog fighters tend to inbreed their dogs rather than cross out to another less game breed, many outcrosses have occurred, either by accident or on purpose, and these dogs have been bred and the offspring registered as purebred.

The Pit Bull is, in fact, a very old and pure breed. Some strains may not be, and many of the "Pit Bulls" involved with dog attacks are in fact mixed breed, and misidentified as APBTs. It is safe to say the Pit Bull is as pure a breed as any registered with the American Kennel Club.

THE "LOCKING JAW"
What the "swelling brain" was to the Doberman breed during its brush with fad panic, the "locking jaw" is to the Pit Bulldog. Any dog's jaw is very strong, and even a good-sized Springer Spaniel can hold its mouth shut against its owner's wishes if it so desires. But no canine is possessed of a "locking jaw." There is no difference called for by breed type. An 80-pound Rottweiler bitch has a head wider than the average APBT, and a large male Rottweiler has a width of head often more than twice as wide as the average Pit Bull. Consequently, the average Rottweiler can bite harder than the average Pit Bull if it wants to. This does not mean that a Rottie can defeat a Pit Bull in a fight (which would be unusual to say the least), but this is only because strength of bite plays a minor role in determining the winner of a dog fight.

When a Pit Bull grasps an object, it can release that object instantly if it wants to, as demonstrated by any trained dog. But because the Pit Bull has been bred for hundreds of generations to grasp cattle (and other animals) and hold on, it has developed a tenacity that is legendary. "Bulldog" is synonymous with tenacity. An APBT, if so inclined, will hold on in play or in all seriousness with a determination not often seen in other breeds. But it is a mistake to believe that all APBTs will grab and hold on when

The "locking jaw" is a common untrue myth associated with the Pit Bull. This is Dread showing healthy tonsils.

Bulldogs are amiable with other animals, contrary to popular belief. This AKC AmStaff. is having a chat with a Dalmatian. Owner, Rick Forman.

with all other dogs that come within his reach. Prejudice against his temper is grossly exaggerated."

As true today as in 1884! While it would be a serious mistake and a gross injustice to the breed ever to underestimate its desire to test its mettle against other dogs, it is just as serious a mistake to underestimate the breed's ability to coexist peacefully with other animals. The determining factors are breeding and training.

A few Pit Bulls are born overly aggressive toward other animals. This is rather rare and is noticeable at a very young age, as young as six or seven weeks. At this time the dog will show a strong interest in challenging other dogs and puppies, and will growl and attempt to stand over other pups and even adult dogs. These pups will also attempt to kill cats and other animals even at this young age. The aggression has nothing to do with gameness, contrary to popular opinion. Some of the gamest fighting dogs in the history of the breed had no desire to fight until placed in a pit, and got along well with other dogs. These dog-aggressive dogs should be destroyed immediately as they are not representative of the breed and can never be trusted to respond with discipline around other animals. Do not mistake normal puppy roughhousing for this unusual behavior—puppies often play rough and hard, and puppies of all breeds get into fights that must be separated by humans, but a pup should not react with aggression to an adult dog. Any young (under eight months) dog that attempts to attack an adult dog should be considered unrepresentative of the breed and destroyed immediately.

The single most important factor in how a Pit Bull will respond to other animals is how the dog has been allowed or expected to respond to them by its owner. Some owners, after reading breed books written by

Gr. Ch. York's Blue Bandit TT U-CD makes friends with a robin. Owner, Ginny York.

This dog, White Rock Dusky Tiger, TT was not raised with cats, but took a protective attitude when introduced to his little pals. Owner, Carla Restivo.

These two friends further dispel the myth that Pit Bulls cannot get along with other animals.

authors who encourage their own dogs to attack and kill other animals, believe this is normal for a Pit Bull. One pamphlet, ironically called "Responsible Pit Bull Ownership" and written in part by a humane society dog-fighting investigator (who has never owned a member of the breed), furthers this unfortunate misinformation by advising Pit Bull owners that, "because of their nature, most Pit Bulls, though raised with other pets, will attack any other dog or cat ...." The pamphlet further encourages owners that "a strong leash must be used whenever the dog is outside where it is normally confined. If you are going to walk your dog around other animals or small children, a muzzle should be considered." Language such as this confirms in the novice Pit Bull owner's mind what the irresponsible dog fighters have been saying—it is okay and to be expected that the dog cannot be controlled around other animals or children. The fact is, even if a dog dislikes other animals or children, he should have strict obedience training and come to understand that any aggressive behavior will not be allowed. This is not unreasonable as evidenced by the thousands of "dominant" breeds (Bullmastiffs, Boxers, Rottweilers, Dobermans, APBTs, Bull Terriers, Fox Terriers, Malamutes, and others) that are brought together in very close range with very delicate show leashes (and no muzzles) at any dog show or obedience trial. Most show dogs are simply never allowed to act aggressively toward other dogs and quickly learn that it will not be tolerated. What a shame that "experts" tell the APBT owner that this cannot be done, and encourage the novice Pit Bull owner to allow their dog to develop into a dog that needs to be walked on a strong leash and with a muzzle.

Like any other "dominant" breed, no adult Pit Bull should be housed with other dogs at an animal shelter. The average APBT is no more aggressive toward other dogs than the average dog of any other "dominant" breed, but he is much more capable of injuring another dog.

Almost all dogs fight for dominance, to establish a

"pecking order." Once a dog has beaten an adversary and that adversary has rolled over and admitted defeat, the dog will let the loser up. Wolves are perfect examples of the natural balance that exists in nature. Wolves live in social groups, consisting of several males and females, yet serious fights are rare. This is because the wolf makes use of the dominance/submission signal system, and the dominant wolf respects the submissive signal of the loser.

In the APBT, man has twisted the dog's instincts for his pleasure, and produced a few members of the breed that no longer understand the submissive gesture. These dogs will not cease fighting, even after their opponent is dead. It is this one fact, and this one fact alone, that makes a few Pit Bulls very dangerous when they are turned against man.

On the other hand, many Pit Bulls coexist very well with other animals. In one Washington state animal shelter an adult female

This Pit Bull looks like he'll protect his raccoon buddy from any roving coonhounds!

A Pit Bull babysits a pair of Canadian geese.

APBT with an unknown history was adopted by the director and allowed to stay in the office during the day. This dog interacts with

AKC Ch. One Stone Berek, SchH III, an American Staffordshire.

strange dogs and cats all day long, and is a gentle and peaceful dog.

My own four dogs, all of which have an intense prey drive, share their yard with over 30 free-roaming guinea pigs, a cat, a dozen or so Old English gamecocks and about 40 bantams. The dogs are often left unattended with all these animals, and all exist peacefully together.

As in any breed of dog, adult males will often fight among themselves. It is uncommon to find adult males of any breed that will tolerate each other if unrestrained. It is no different with the Pit Bull. Adult females, also, will often fight among themselves in an attempt to establish dominance. Though the severity of the fighting may be greater with the APBT, the instances of fights among Pit Bulls and other "dominant" type breeds are similar. When housing or handling APBTs with an unknown history, the animal-control officer should take the same precautions that they would take when handling any other dog around other animals. As most people know, a large percentage of dogs from any breed will kill cats if given the chance. The same should be assumed of the Pit Bull breed. But once an APBT has proven itself to be trustworthy around a cat, there is no reason to assume that it will suddenly become aggressive without cause.

PIT BULLS ATTACK WITHOUT WARNING

Like any myth, there is a kernel of truth behind this oversimplification. "Warning" is another word for threat display, which is an important part of animal behavior and is used to

Is this Pit Bull getting ready to hook up his sled team?

Ch. Spartan's Zoanna CD, U-CD, owned by Teresa Ewing.

keep fighting to a minimum. If one wolf is eating, and another approaches, the eating wolf will exhibit a threat display, warning the other wolf to stay away. When the approaching wolf respects the threat display and backs off, a potentially dangerous fight has been avoided, which helps maintain pack cohesion. Threat displays save a lot of wear and tear on the animal world and play an important part in the dog-human relationship also. While man has lived with the dog for thousands of years, we are still not terribly adept at reading dogs' warning signals. How many people understand that a dog holding very still, standing across their path, is exhibiting as sure a sign of warning as a growl?

While all Pit Bulls do give some warning that they are going to attack, the ability or desire to make prolonged threat displays has been bred down in many strains of this breed. A threat display is a waste of time in a dog that earns its living by fighting—its owner wants it to jump right in and get the fight over with, not spend time circling and warning its opponent. For this reason dogs which minimized their threat display were used for breeding. Eventually a dog was produced which, when set down in a pit, would rush its opponent immediately and begin the fight without engaging in warning behavior.

Outside of the pit situation, APBTs do engage in minimal threat displays when faced with other dogs. Because many APBTs seem to enjoy getting in a scrap, they do not seek to warn their opponent away, but rather would get right down to business. For this reason, it is a good idea always to restrain an unknown Pit Bull away from other dogs, and not to allow them even to sniff noses. Once an APBT has decided to engage an opponent, it will grasp the dog with surprising speed and intensity, catching the uninitiated completely off guard.

When facing the human opponent, though, the Pit Bull shows a much greater incidence of warning behavior. Because the Pit Bull has never been bred to regard the human as an opponent (such as guard dog breeds have), the breed responds quite differently when attacking a human. The average APBT feels an intimidation when faced with a human opponent which it does not feel when faced with another dog. Because of this intimidation it will be much

Cheek's Red Baroness, SchH III, U-UD, with her mother, Cory.

Above left: Ch. Knockout's Patriot Missile, U-CD, BH, CGC, SchH I (OFA). *Above right:* Dr. Rudy Kasni's Young AmStaff "Jan" a rugged looking bitch with great character. *Below:* Three fabulous working bitches owned by Annetta Cheek—Little Bit, U-CD; Vicki; and Baroness, U-UD, SchH II.

Red Kelly and Baby Butch owned by Dennis and Zuni Saccher.

After a nice walk in the woods, Bandog Dread pauses by his truck. Note his personalized license plate and custom welded wire canopy to keep him cool in the summer.

Balancing Act. Bill Bombader with "Stratton" in New York. Can your dog do this?

more likely to display threat behavior because it would like to avoid the fight if possible. In these cases the dog will look like any other dog, barking, hair up, growling and showing other manifestations of fear. The one exception to this would be a well-trained attack dog, who, regardless of breed, will have been conditioned to fearlessly attack a human. The American Staffordshire Terrier, "Benjamin," seen on national television news attacking a Los Angeles area animals control officer in the mid-80s, was a trained protection dog, and watching this dog one can see the calm determination of a trained dog ordered to attack.

When any dog of any breed means business about attacking a human, it will not engage in an extensive threat display. The old myth that "barking dogs don't bite" has a kernel of truth in it. A dog engaged in a threat display is not as apt to bite you as a dog that is not engaged in a threat display. Not all dogs that mean business will engage in a

B.W. Lightsey's Search and Rescue dog, "Puller," works out in Schutzhund.

threat display; some will engage in a very abbreviated one which is often difficult to recognize.

PIT BULLS HAVE 2,000 POUNDS PER SQUARE INCH (PSI) BITE PRESSURE

Back in the mid-'70s, during the Doberman/guard dog fad panic, the very first figures on bite strength appeared from out of nowhere, with no explanation of how they were obtained. At that time the German Shepherd was credited with having 400 PSI and Dobermans were said to have anywhere from 600 to 1200 PSI bite pressure. In reality, and any professional "decoy" (the person who takes the bites in police/Schutzhund/attack dog training) can tell you, the Doberman ranks as one of the softest biting of the guard-dog breeds.

When the Pit Bull became the next fad-panic breed, authors lost no time in assigning a host of totally arbitrary numbers to them. Wolves, too, were given an imaginary PSI, so that the APBT could be assigned a higher one! Anywhere from 600 to 2,000 PSI has been credited to the breed, yet no one has ever been able to document where these readings are coming from.

In reality there has never been *any* scientific reading taken, and *any* measurement of a dog's bite would apply only for that particular dog, and not for a whole breed. As a breed, the Pit Bull varies a great deal in size. A 45-pound dog will not be able to grasp nearly as hard as a 65-pound dog. And a dog's bite

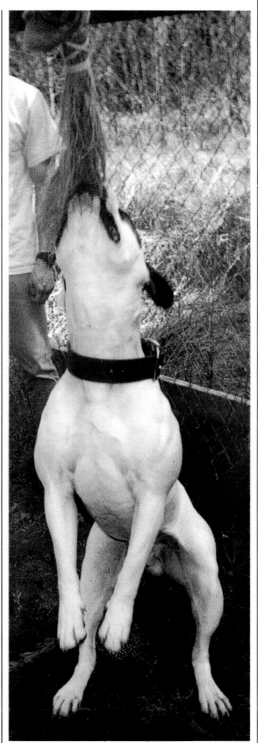

"Bite pressure" is a mythical term associated with Pit Bulls that has yet to be documented. This American Bulldog is owned by Tom Dubat.

AKC Ch. Indian Rein's Animal, CD, SchH I, TT provides a resting place for a young friend. Owner, Jeanette Durand.

intensity will vary greatly with its emotional state and depend even more on what "drive" it is in when it bites.

For instance, a 65-pound dog that is biting on command, with little frustration and in defense drive, will bite probably a third as hard as a 50-pound dog that has been very frustrated and is working in a prey drive. (Prey drive is equivalent to hunting drive. "Defense drive" is equivalent to self-defense drive.)

The author has over 18 years of experience taking bites during training from all manner of dogs and can state with complete authority that no one breed bites harder than another, though some large breeds such as Rottweilers and Akitas tend to have a much harder bite than smaller Shepherds and

Dobermans, if all other factors are the same. The Pit Bull is much more tenacious but does not have the strongest jaw strength.

THE PIT BULL IS THE STRONGEST BREED IN THE WORLD

Perhaps because the average Pit Bull can defeat a dog of any other breed, even those several times its size, all sorts of "super canine" attributes have been credited to him. Perhaps it is easier for the owner of a 130-pound Akita or Rottweiler to assume that somehow the Pit Bull is physically different from other dogs, and that is why a 50-pound APBT can easily defeat the larger dogs. But the Pit Bull differs in no qualitative or quantitative way from any other dog. When the APBT does an incredible physical feat, you can be sure that his heart and mind had more to do with it than a superior physical ability.

Is the Bulldog the strongest breed in the world? One must define "strongest." At a weight pulling event for dogs, there are always two prizes given. The first is for the dog who pulled the most weight of any dog at the event. The second prize is given to the dog who pulled the most weight in proportion to how much the dog weighed. Smaller dogs can always pull more per pound of body weight then larger dogs. But larger dogs can always pull more

Pit Bulls are excellent pullers for their size, but are far from matching the strength of larger breeds such as the Mastiff. Owner, Carla Restivo.

overall weight. The author has personally witnessed dogs weighing between 140 to 175 pounds pull over 5,000 pounds on a wheeled cart for International Weight Pull Association world records. The dogs that pull the most weight overall are generally pure or mixed-breed Malamutes, Saint Bernards, Great Danes or Mastiffs. Pit Bulls do well in these contests, especially the very small ones weighing 35 pounds or less. But it cannot be said that the APBT dominates the sport in any sense, and many good APBTs are beaten by very strong and game pulling dogs of numerous breeds. While a few outstanding and professionally conditioned Pit Bulls could probable defeat any other dog close to their size, it cannot be said that the Pit Bull is stronger than any other breed overall. The power of the Bulldog comes primarily from his heart and his gameness, not any unusual configuration of his muscles.

Baroness, U-CDX, SchH III, shows typical bulldog athleticism as she takes the utility bar jump.

Bandog Dread working out. Dread has earned the IWPA "Working Dog Superior" title.

The Pit Bull can be developed into a superb athlete and has a determination of mind that enables him to perform some astounding physical feats not often accomplished by other breeds. Fortunately, the breed is often owned by people who are attracted to the dog's rugged good looks and athletic abilities, and who encourage their dogs to stay in top shape by a rigorous exercise program rarely used by owners of other breeds.

BULLETS BOUNCE OFF THE PIT BULL'S BODY

During the Doberman fad panic there were many reports of bullets bouncing off this breed as well. Of course, bullets can strike any living body in such a way that they bounce off, and dogs happen to have a very thin covering of flesh over their skulls, so the chance that a small caliber bullet will bounce off the head of a dog is increased.

The skull of an APBT is in no way any thicker or stronger or more "bullet proof" than any other breed.

THE PIT BULL KILLS MORE PEOPLE IN PROPORTION TO ITS POPULATION

The population of the Pit Bull has never been accurately determined by anyone. Those who are interested in making it appear

Pit Bull working in obedience training.

that the breed has killed large numbers of humans in proportion to its population have relied upon the number of registered dogs, often using only one registering body! One often-quoted report determined the frequency of bites for all APBTs and their crosses by using the number of AKC-registered *Bull Terriers,* a rare breed indeed! Some reports have used the number of AKC-registered American Staffordshire Terriers. The Am. Staff is another breed which has never gained much popularity.

The truth is, during the mid to late '80's alone, there were hundreds of thousands of APBTs registered with the UKC and the ADBA. Hundreds of thousands more were never registered. It is safe to assume that for every purebred Pit Bulldog there are three or four times that many cross-bred dogs. If all these dogs had been compared to AKC registration numbers, the "Pit Bull" as defined by the press would have easily reached the "top ten" in popularity, making its incidence of biting ridiculously small compared to such breeds as huskies, German Shepherds, Labradors and Cocker Spaniels.

Considering the fact that the Pit Bull was exploited by drug dealers, punks, dog fighters and others who encouraged anti-social and dangerous behavior in the dogs, it is a testimony to the breed that more people were not injured during these sad days for the breed.

Regardless of what the press reports, the breed of dog responsible for the most human fatalities year after year is not the APBT.

A DOG THAT IS "GAME" IS DOG-AGGRESSIVE AND WANTS TO FIGHT

"Game, " defined in terms of a dog's behavior, means the characteristic of not quitting. In a fighting dog, this means a dog that will continue to cross the pit, even on broken and mutilated limbs, in order to finish a fight. Gameness is not exclusive to dog fighting, nor is a dog fight the only way to ascertain how game a dog is. Gameness does not mean a desire to fight—it means a desire to finish or succeed at a task. Therefore, a dog can display

The Pit Bull has been unfairly and unjustly categorized as a "killer" dog by the media. This is "Stratton," owned by Bill Bombader.

gameness at any task it is asked to do.

A few examples of true gameness in a dog would be the weight-pull dog that simply never quits trying to pull a load, and must be stopped by his handler when the load becomes brush or debris hour after hour searching for victims. All these are tests of gameness with value (unlike dog fighting, which has no value to society whatsoever) and acceptance in our modern world. Anyone who values his dog cares little if his dog is "dead

Gameness is tested and proven in many areas outside the fighting pit. Here a Pit Bull qualifies at a utility obedience trial.

too heavy, the tracking dog who continues to work out a faint, hours-old trail in the 100°F heat and scores a perfect 100 in a grueling German F.H. tracking test, a Schutzhund dog who works in the blazing sun, doing courage test after courage test in order to train new trial decoys, until he is stopped for fear of heatstroke, the search and rescue dog who climbs over game" (will work until it dies) for this has no practical application in today's working dog either. A dog need only be game enough to complete a task to the best of its ability. We can ask no more of our working dogs than we can ask of ourselves.

Old-time fighting dogs were often quite docile around other dogs outside a pit situation, and this makes sense. A dog confident enough to win in the pit would not view another dog as a threat, thus he would not feel it necessary to make a threat display whenever he saw another dog. Only dogs which are insecure and feel they must challenge every other dog will react with aggression to the sight of another dog. The ideal Pit Bull is confident enough in himself that he refrains from threat displays in any circumstance. If challenged he will respond, but even then with minimal threat display. It is safe to assume that an APBT lunging at the end of its lead, snarling and growling at another dog feels threatened and is therefore responding with a threat display designed to frighten the other dog off. This is not a sign of gameness at all, but rather one of poor nerves.

Gr. Ch. Guerra's Beringer, BH, CGC, U-CD, OFA begins to track. Tracking is another competition which tests a bulldog's gameness.

Ch. Panda's Gallant Boss, TT, CD, U-CD, BH, CGC, OFA owned by Cindy Herron.

Choosing a Bulldog

Hopefully you will acquire a Pit Bull *after* much careful thought and research, not impulsively when first confronted with a wiggly puppy with warm brown eyes! Remember that a dog represents a huge commitment on your part: a commitment of time, energy and money. A dog may be with you for the next 15 years of your life. You may be in a position to have a dog now, but where will you be in five years? There are many things to consider before you even decide to purchase a dog. More than half the dogs purchased as pets end up given away, dead, or euthanized at an

Purchase a Pit Bull only after careful thought and research. These two AmStaffs are owned by Carla Restivo.

animal shelter before the age of four years. In order to avoid this tragedy, please consider the following reasons/excuses people give to animal shelter workers

finding housing that allows a dog is nearly impossible in some parts of the country. Many times the dog ends up being euthanized at the local animal

The decision to buy a dog should be made by those who are firmly settled in their home. This is York's Bullseye, a UKC-registered female.

when turning their pets in, and think about how they may apply to you.

Buying A Dog Before Settled: Many young people purchase a pet before they are established and the experience ends up a tragedy for both themselves and the dog. Starting a career many times means relocating, and

shelter due to the lack of rental homes available which allow dogs.

Having to Move: Many people do not realize just how difficult it is to move and find a place to rent which allows pets. Many people are forced to move and have very little time to try and find a home for their dog. It is very difficult to

The blue color of this pup's eyes will change to a darker color as it matures. Blue eyes are unusual and not desirable in APBTs.

find an appropriate, loving home for an adult dog.

Buying a Dog as a Gift: People who buy an older relative a dog as a watchdog or companion often find that the person has no interest in or ability to care for a dog. Buying a dog as a gift for anyone is a bad idea. If a person wants a dog, he will get his own dog! (A Pit Bull is not an appropriate pet for an elderly person in any case, due to their extensive exercise requirements.)

Can't Afford: One of the most common reasons for giving up a pet is the owner's not realizing just how much money it takes to maintain a dog. Many people seem to think that owning a pet is a right, instead of a luxury, and do not realize that they alone are responsible for veterinary costs. Your local vet charges a fair price for a service rendered; they are under no obligation to offer spay/ neuter or other services at a

reduced rate. If you cannot afford the cost of proper veterinarian care you cannot afford to own a pet. The prospective Bulldog owner should talk to a local vet before purchasing a pup, and have the necessary money set aside for puppy shots, worming and possible emergencies. Remember, there is no such thing as a free pet—they all cost the same to maintain. The purchase price of a pup is just the tip of the iceberg where costs are concerned.

Time Requirement: The average age of a dog being turned into the animal shelter by its owner is ten months. Many thoughtless people purchase a puppy only to find that the puppy matures into a large, powerful

Be sure you can afford the maintenance and veterinary costs of a dog before purchasing one. This is "Charo," SchH I, owned by Frank Sulky.

animal that makes demands upon their time. A dog as physical as the Pit Bull requires extra effort and time, and the prospective owner should ask himself the following questions: Do I come right home from work, or do I like to stop off at the club for a couple of hours? Do I come home and stay home or do I go right out again for the evening? Am I busy every weekend or can I devote three or four hours on the weekend to my dog's mental and physical well being? Perhaps you will find that your schedule would

Decide whether your lifestyle and schedule would be fair to a dog before you decide to get one.

be unfair to a dog. Better to find that out now than when the dog is ten months old and difficult to place in a new home.

Please think long and hard before you make your decision. The Pit Bull is a unique breed, requiring unique commitments of time and energy. Some breeds are content with a "couch potato" lifestyle, but the Bulldog thrives on work and companionship. If you find that you have the time, money, lifestyle and energy for a Bulldog, you will find it well worth it.

PUPPY OR ADULT?
Should you purchase a small puppy, or should you bring a slightly older dog into your home? Most people prefer the close bonding that occurs when a small pup is bought. The obvious advantage of a puppy is the opportunity to enjoy the joyful puppy stage. The pup will be able to be better shaped into the kind of dog you desire, though hereditary predisposition will limit your ability to some extent. For instance, a puppy which is born with a temperament problem such as shyness may be able to be modified behaviorally but will always have a tendency to be shy. In extreme cases, no matter how the dog is trained or socialized, the shy puppy will develop into a shy adult. That is why it is so important to see the parents and as many other relatives of the pup you plan to purchase as possible.

There are advantages to an older dog also. You can tell exactly what the dog will end up

Above: Sagebrush Tacoma Danni, owned by Carla Restivo. **Below:** P.R. Pittaway's Red Baron, a ten-year-old Pit Bull.

Once you decide to purchase a dog, you must determine whether you want an adult or a puppy. This is a blue brindle pup.

looking like, which is important for persons interested in showing in conformation. You can avoid the destructive puppy stage by bringing home an older dog, but you also run the risk of bringing home another person's problem dog. Beware of the unscrupulous owner who, in an attempt to dump his dog on an unsuspecting party, may keep quiet about a dog's behavioral problems. The older dog is a good candidate for a single person who works and doesn't want to keep a puppy confined all day while out working. One thing to remember about buying an adult dog—if it is a truly good dog, why are the owners getting rid of it? If it is a retired show dog, has the dog been a house pet or has the dog been kenneled?

Prices of pups are generally higher than prices of adults; adult dogs are much harder to place in a home, and usually the owner is willing to give the dog away free. Puppies also represent a much higher outlay in initial vet fees, as they will need worming as well as a series of vaccinations.

There is a risk involved in bringing any adult dog into a family with children. Dogs of any breed can be frightened or aggressive with children, and it is never a good idea to allow any dog which has not been raised around children to be unsupervised around them. When there are children in the home it is preferable to introduce a puppy into the family.

While a puppy represents a great deal of commitment in time, an adult dog brings the element of surprise into the first few days of getting to know one another. Do you leave the dog alone in the house? What will he do? Will you come home to a shredded couch? A puppy can generally be depended on to be destructive, but an older dog can do much more damage!

It should be mentioned here that the local animal shelter is not the proper place to look for a Pit Bull. Dogs purchased from animal shelters have little or no known history, and this increases the risk of getting a problem dog. Also, dogs which end up in an animal shelter have almost always had substandard owners (who allowed them to show up there in the first place), so it is fair to guess that the animal has also had a less than perfect upbringing and medical history. Purchase your pup after carefully considering all the facts. A shelter animal, while possibly turning out to be a very nice dog, may also turn out to be a very terrible mistake.

A cute Tacoma-bred Am. Staff. shows early prey drive. Owner, Carla Restivo.

MALE OR FEMALE
Male dogs are generally larger, stronger and more impressive looking than a female. Males lift their legs to urinate, killing

This pup is from the "Blue Bully" line.

shrubs and flowers. They are often more aggressive toward other animals. They are more prone to leave the area if they get loose. Whenever statistics of dogs "in trouble" are tallied, almost all dogs involved in bites, livestock killing and other nuisance complaints are males. Males are often more sensitive and "soft" to the owner, tending to "toe the line" more easily. Males are often described as being more eager to please.

Female dogs (bitches) are smaller and easier to handle. They urinate on the ground, killing the lawn instead of the bushes. They are often just as aggressive as males toward other animals, particularly toward other bitches. Bitches are rarely involved in severe bite situations. They are often more tolerant of children, and tend to bond with the family better than an unaltered male. They can be real "bitches"

You may want to have your Pit Bull's ears cropped. This is an example of ear-wrapping after cropping.

most, and will return from the vet her little happy self. Almost all dogs have to be physically restrained from being overactive after spay surgery; they recover very quickly. Once a bitch has been spayed she will not come into "heat," and will not bleed or become attractive to male dogs. Since bitches only breed when they are in heat, she will resist any effort on the part of a male to breed her. She will be incapable of producing a litter. For the pet owner the spay surgery is heaven-sent and means an end to howling males outside the door, messy spots on the couch and rug, and unwanted litters of pups. Spaying a bitch does not appear to produce any changes in temperament or ability.

A perfectly built young male bred by Dr. Annetta Cheek.

Does altering a dog somehow lessen its abilities or worth? The answer is No! Many serious working dogs are altered so that heat cycles and sex drive do not interfere with their work. Many top competition dogs in Schutzhund, obedience and weight pull are altered, as are many dogs working for the police and customs departments. By removing the sex drive, the other important working drives can be utilized to their fullest without distraction.

SHOW, PET OR WORKING?
Just exactly what do you want most from your dog? Do you have plans to spend your evenings going for long peaceful walks? Do you want a dog to go fishing with you? Do you want a dog that will compete at a top level in international weight-pulling competitions? Do you want a dog with strong drives for Schutzhund or obedience? Do you want to buy a puppy with the best chance of developing into a show-quality dog? These are all things to consider before you choose your pup, as they have important bearing on the price you will pay, the breeders you will choose from and the drives you will look for in the puppy's parents and relatives. Is it possible to get "the perfect puppy," the one that will turn into a show champion and also be

This bulldog pup receives an inoculation. A regular schedule of vaccinations should be set up with your vet.

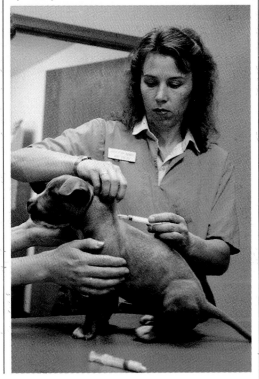

capable of being a top-rate working dog? You can, but it is wise to determine what your priorities are, and choose your dog in accordance with that. If your heart lies with conformation showing, purchase a dog from the best show lines you can afford, and hope it has the soundness and drives to do work. If your heart lies with the working dog, you will get the best results from choosing a dog specifically on the drives of the breeding stock it comes from, and disregard color and the finer points of the written conformation standard.

A SHOW DOG

If your goal is to purchase a pup which will finish as a champion, you must decide if you are going to get rid of the dog and start over if it fails to develop properly. If your goal is truly to finish a champion, and you live where the competition is tough, you may have to go through several dogs in order to find one that can win. Or, do you want to

Gr. Ch. PR Tyee's Boy Bosworth U-CD, enjoying the water.

If you are intent on showing a dog, you must be especially wise when choosing your pup. This is PR Nelson's Aja.

keep your fingers crossed and hope for the best, keeping the dog no matter what happens?

If you are inclined to keep buying pups until you find a winner, you are best off to buy from a breeder which offers a guarantee on replacing a pup with another if the first one fails to finish. Be advised, most of these guarantees insist that you give the first dog back to the breeder, a thing many pet owners are loathe to do. It is hard to give up a pup you have raised simply because of the set of the ears, or the turn of the stifle. You can see why it is so very important to choose wisely when purchasing your pup. The decision you make should result in a dog which will be with you for the next several years.

What do you look for in a show puppy? There is no easy way to tell how a pup will turn out as an adult. Experienced breeders can

the same family of dogs has been bred to produce the litter. The pedigree will reflect several relatives being bred together, not close enough to be in-bred (like father-daughter) but enough so that the names of two or three dogs should appear multiple times. The following is an example of a line-bred pedigree:

Colby's Wally

Colby's Jessie

Colby's Prince

Colby's Pumpsie

Colby's Winnie

Colby's Molly

Colby's Emjay

Colby's Jill

Colby's Mink

Colby's Prince

Colby's Pumpsie

Colby's Winnie

Deman's Jet

Orday's Smokey

Lopay's Monkey

A hardworkingPR Cheek's Red Baroness, SchH III, U-UD, at rest.

Line-breeding assures you that the dogs have a better chance of being uniform in appearance than a "scatter-bred" litter does. Scatter-bred means completely unrelated dogs are bred together. Scatter-bred dogs are often, like mongrels, healthier and less prone to temperament and genetic problems. But like a mongrel, they rarely are able to reproduce their unique qualities when bred. Breeding two scatter-bred dogs together will produce a litter of purebreds, but the littermates may vary widely in appearance and temperament.

The practice of in-breeding dogs is controversial. Many people feel that in-bred dogs run the risk of being born with health or mental problems. The fact is an in-bred dog is as good or as bad as the dogs from which it is produced. Many breeds of animals used in agriculture, such as beef cattle, dairy cattle and certain types of sheep, have been developed by in-breeding. The only problems that occur with in-breeding dogs is that the dog breeder is often more

By all means ask to see the pedigree before you purchase a Pit Bull you intend to show. These are PR Corlander Redberry, PR Cheek's Red Baroness, and Foxy.

emotionally attached to their creations, and therefore less likely to cull poor results, as a farmer would do. Whatever traits the parents shared, such as a hyper temperament, bowed legs or a beautiful head, are going to be "set" in the offspring because of the doubling up of the genes. Health problems do seem to occur more often in in-bred pups simply because if the parents are carrying the problem, the pups will manifest it. The following is an example of a tightly in-bred litter.

                                        Bryson's Satan

                    Hemphill's Geronimo

                                        Hemphill's Rebel

        Wilder's Geronimo II

                                        Bryson's Satan

                    Hemphill's Red Dixie

                                        Hemphill's Rebel

Jerome's Hemphill Maud

                                        Bryson's Satan

                    Hemphill's Geronimo

                                        Hemphill's Rebel

        Spearman's Scarlet Lady

                                        Bryson's Satan

                    Hemphill's Red Dixie

                                        Hemphill's Rebel

If you decide on a scatter-bred dog, realize that the pup you choose may or may not grow up to closely resemble its parents in appearance or temperament. If you decide on a line-bred pup, there is a better than average chance the dog will resemble and act like its parents. If you buy an in-bred pup, you had

very scrupulous about the inherent conditions that their dogs could carry is doing you and the breed a disservice.

A PET DOG
Choosing a pet to provide you and your family with a lifetime of companionship and protection is no less a job than choosing a

Double Trouble, a fawn bitch.

better be happy with what the parents both look and act like, for that is probably what you will get. When buying an in-bred pup, you must be especially careful to be sure that the parents are free of congenital health problems such as hip dysplasia, thyroid problems and other genetic defects. A breeder who in-breeds without being

dog for show or working purposes. A family dog must have a faultless temperament, as he is exposed to a variety of everyday stresses and strains. He must be sturdy and sound and pleasing in appearance.
What defines a dog as a "pet"-quality dog? Does this mean it is somehow a lesser dog than its "show" -quality brothers and

Gr. Ch. Hardroc Cafe has some fun time with his pups.

sisters? Is there something wrong with it?

The term "show quality" is often misleading. Labelling a dog "show quality" seems to suggest that it is somehow superior to its littermates in all ways. This may not be so. The term show quality simply means that, in the opinion of the breeder, this dog can be shown in conformation, and has a chance of attaining its championship. The dog physically conforms to the written standard of the breed, and should have no major disqualifying faults such as a crooked bite, long, curled tail or bowed legs. Show quality *does not*

A large male APBT of Archer bloodlines.

mean that the dog is any smarter, sounder or healthier.

The person who breeds for show quality can obtain a higher price for those pups which appear to be show quality from other people interested in showing their dog. A person looking for a show dog may pay $500.00 for a dog which is not nearly as outgoing and friendly as its sister or brother who do not conform to the written standard as closely. This is why the person interested in obtaining a family pet would be well advised to pay less and get the pet puppy.

Some breeders charge the same price for all their pups, since they realize that show quality is, after all, a bit of a misrepresentation at eight weeks of age. Be honest with the breeder about what you want in a dog. If your intentions are breeding, then you should buy a breeder-quality dog, and not a pet-quality dog. Bear in mind that a breeder who has never shown a dog cannot possibly have the experience to determine if his pups are show quality.

The things you would look for in a pet puppy would be an outgoing but not hyper temperament, good health and no hint of shyness. While a show or working quality pup may grow up and not fulfill its destiny as a show or working dog, a well-picked pet puppy can rarely fail to grow into a loved and valued family member!

THE WORKING/SPORT DOG
What you would look for in a working prospect would be determined a great deal by what work or sport you want the dog to

Careful consideration comes into play when picking a Pit Bull puppy. This new owner seems to have walked away with a wise choice.

do. The traits needed for a first-rate therapy dog are not necessarily those needed for a narcotics-detection dog. The only general rules of thumb when looking for a working/sport pup are these:

• try to get a pup from proven working/sport lines

• make sure the parents are sound and certified against hip dysplasia

• make sure the parents have the drives you want in your dog

• pick the most outgoing and stable pup—no matter how he looks

You should know what drives you need for the work/sport you intend to do, and look for dogs which display large amounts of those same drives. For search and rescue (SAR) you need an athletic dog with very low dog aggression

Above: Gr. Ch. York's Blue Bandit TT, U-CD, and owner Ginny York. **Below:** *A little Pit Bull owned by Tom Dubat.*

Bandog Grip at six weeks. She later became only the second Pit Bull in the world to earn a Herding Instinct Certificate (Dread was the first).

and a high prey drive. For obedience you need a dog with high prey drive and a very "up" attitude. For Schutzhund you need extreme prey drive coupled with an athletic body and good, strong nerves. For herding you need strong prey/herding drives coupled with a dog that can listen and stay calm while working. For tracking you need strong prey drive and determination. For weight pulling you look for strong prey drive, determination, absolute soundness and willingness to please. The therapy dog needs strong nerves, an outgoing but sensible nature and a real love of people.

Depending on how seriously you take your training, you may be able to find a dog you will be happy with in any average litter. Instead of looking for physical perfection, the working dog handler will be looking only at temperament and drives. It is difficult to say for certain just how temperament and drives will be manifested in the adult dog. Some pups show little or no prey drive as pups, only to become "ball-crazy" adults. Some pups will show great promise as a pup only to become gun-shy as an adult. It is just as much a gamble as picking a show pup. And like picking a

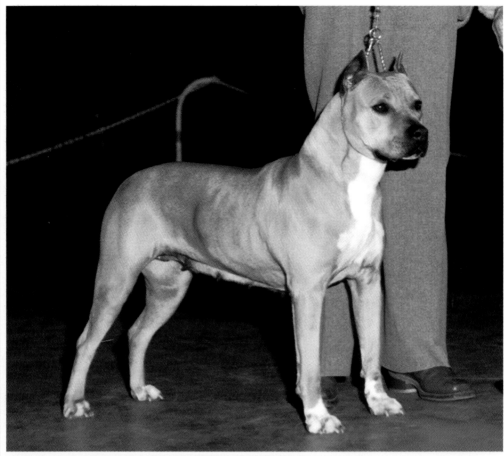

AKC Ch. and UKC Gr. Ch. Estrella's Rujita De Fraja, CDX. This bulldog, owned by Estrella Kennels, is dual-registered as an American Staffordshire and an APBT.

show pup, the working pup should come from a breeder who specializes in the work you want to do. A person who does not compete or train for work/sport cannot possibly assist you in choosing a work/sport pup. Some show or obedience breeders will point to a growling, aggressive pup in a litter and state that this animal is the best Schutzhund prospect, even though they know nothing about Schutzhund and don't understand that a growling puppy is showing weak nerves, not courage. If you are not sure what to look for, ask a person familiar with the breed and with the training to assist you.

Very often in this breed it is possible to find great working potential dogs in a show-bred litter. Don't worry much about where your working prospect comes from—if it is a good dog it is a good dog, no matter where it came from. There is a persistent rumor that working/sport dogs are usually ugly dogs, or dogs which couldn't make it as show dogs. There is not a descending order of value of dogs in a litter, with show quality at the top and

A litter of blue brindle pups.

A seven-week-old bulldog pup can get into endless trouble.

pet or working at the bottom. To a work/sport person, the pretty show-quality pup with no drives or lacking in temperament may seem the worst of the lot and worthy of being culled from the litter, while its uglier littermate with strong drives and nerves may command a very dear price. In some European countries, true working dogs are never registered—it is considered the surest way to ruin the working ability of the dogs. This is because too much emphasis is put on breeding only to registered dogs, and not to the best dogs. If, for instance, an outstanding dog is purebred yet not registered, the true working-dog breeder would not hesitate to utilize the dog at the price of not having registered dogs. That is the special appeal of the work/sport dog: his beauty is in what he does, not how he looks doing it!

One word of caution: while the ugly little pup may be the outstanding pup in the litter from a work/sport point of view, do not ever compromise soundness. More than any other dog, the work/sport dog must be sound, and good conformation usually indicates a certain degree of soundness. And remember that first and foremost comes temperament—pick the bold, friendly, outgoing pup which never growls or barks at your approach, and who is first to greet you.

A Dynamite Kennels litter of red Pit Bulls take a tubby together.

Three red/red-nose pups at play. There is no standard color in APBT conformation.

INSIDE OR OUTSIDE DOG?

Should your dog stay inside, outside or have access to both? The Pit Bull makes a great house dog, and with its short coat is best kept inside in cooler climates. They are neat and shed very little, and their smaller size makes them welcome in the smallest home. Why get a dog if it is going to be kept outside, away from the family? The dog will be lonely and you will not benefit from its protection or company. Also, dogs kept outside are never as intelligent or socialized as those who partake of family life.

All dogs need plenty of time outside though, especially in good weather, and the house Bulldog should have access to a securely fenced yard area. Never tether an APBT outside without a protective fence around the perimeter to protect it from dog thieves, mischievous children and from getting into trouble with loose dogs. For the ultimate in convenience for your dog, a doggy-door from the inside of the house to a secure kennel area outside is great.

If you must keep your Bulldog outside, spend time on making his quarters as comfortable and secure as possible. The Pit Bull

Carla Restivo's outstanding dog houses feature two rooms, windows, and a sunning porch.

A kennel run adequate for holding a dog for short periods. Notice the protective roof and cedar chips on the floor.

requires a well-insulated dog house in colder climates, it has very thin hair. While a dog may survive a winter in an inadequate dog house, that doesn't mean it isn't miserable the whole time.

The best setup for a Pit Bull that must be kept outside is a large chain-link kennel, at least 20 feet by 8 feet. This should have a solid top on it to keep out the weather and sun, and for sanitation reasons should have a solid concrete slab floor. Inside should be a solid and insulated dog house filled with straw or clean blankets, and a deep bucket of fresh water. A resting platform, such as a pallet with a solid side with a blanket or piece of carpet on it, should provide a place for the dog to get up off the cement when it doesn't want to lie in its dog house.

Whether a dog is kept inside or outside, it requires a good stiff walk everyday, and time spent in the company of its owner. No dog should be expected to live its life out sitting in a dog house away from people. If you plan on keeping a dog outside the majority of the time, ask yourself, "Why do I really want a dog anyway?"

REGISTRATION PAPERS

When a puppy is said to have "papers," it means that both of his parents are registered with

Above: Gr. Ch. Our Gang Ca Spatz at four months. He became the foundation stud for Dynamite Kennels. Below: "Ziggy," a six-month-old Pit Bull, rests in the yard.

Above: Pit Bulls love the water, swim well, and are natural retrievers. Below: An adult male APBT with a brindle pup.

the same registering body, and you can therefore theoretically trace his ancestry back several generations. Papers are helpful to the show breeder, as they let the breeder see what type of dogs the pup has descended from, which tells them with what type of dog this one should be bred to, to produce the kind of pups they are looking to produce. Papers are less important to the pet and working/sport dog handler, who choose their dog on *its* qualities, not the qualities of its ancestors.

There is often a great deal of confusion regarding papers, and many times puppy buyers find out too late that the pup they recently purchased is not, in fact, registrable. There are a few steps

Always insist on seeing the registration papers of your dog's parents. York's Ruffian Gator, AKC–and UKC-registered.

you can take to keep potential problems from arising when you purchase a "papered" pup.

1) Always insist on seeing the registration papers on *both* parents, and note down the registration number and name of both dogs.

2) Make sure the papers for both parents are from the same registry.

3) If the breeder does not have

the puppy papers available when you pick the pup up, get a statement in writing as to when you can expect the papers to arrive.

4) As soon as you get your puppy's papers, fill them out correctly and send them in.

A good breeder will send for the registeration papers soon after the puppy's birth, and have them on hand when potential buyers come

Above: *Make sure the parents of your pup are from the same registry. This eight week old APBT pup explores his new home.* **Below:** *"Dixie," "Spanky," and "Buster," all owned by Steve Wendelin.*

to see the pups. Dealing with a breeder which does this is the single best way to avoid problems. Sometimes, though, the registering body can be quite slow in returning papers, and there can be a delay which is no fault of the breeders.

With AKC papers, the breeder has the opportunity to name the pup and the new owner cannot change that name. The AKC breeder also has the choice of not naming the pup, thus leaving it up to the new owner. Once the pup is named, either way, it can never be changed. The UKC breeder has no control over the dog's name once they sign over the papers. The new owner can change the dog's name as often as they wish, until the dog becomes a champion (at that time it cannot

be changed again). This has led to some real confusion when tracing pedigrees!

When you receive your puppy papers, the dog will be listed as being owned by the breeder. You will need to send them in yourself to get the dog listed in your name. At this time you can request a pedigree, which will show you several generations of your dog's ancestors.

A WORD ABOUT FRAUD

In any registry there is a certain amount of error in many pedigrees. It is not uncommon for unethical breeders to put down the name of a well-known stud dog when in reality some other dog sired the litter. Another common practice with large kennels is when two or three bitches have pups near the same time, all the pups will be registered as coming from the best dogs in the kennel so as to increase their sale value. No one registry has more fraud than another, and any fraud is not the fault of the registry but rather entirely of the unethical breeder.

Teresa Ewing's working dogs. Seated are PR Timberline's Rocky, TDI, U-CD; PR Timberline's Humbug, U-CD; PR Timberline's Ms. Morgan, TDI, U-CD; and PR Ch. Timberline's Chance. Down are PR Timberline's Nyssa, TDI, U-CD; PR Ch. Timberline's Maggie, TDI, U-CD; PR Timberline's Ms. Fortune, U-CD; and Ch. Spartan's Zoanna, TDI, U-CD.

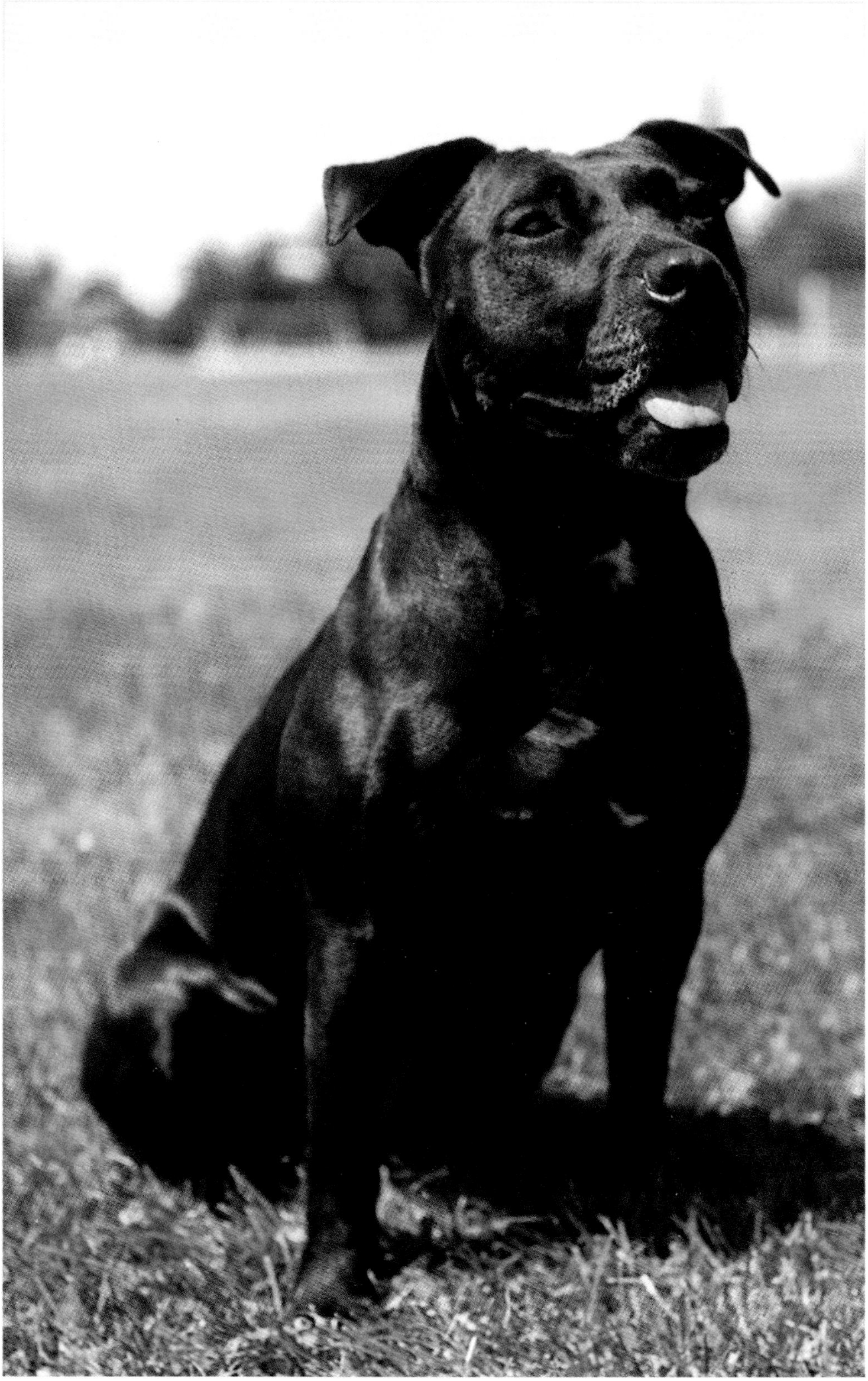

The Working Pit Bull

NARCOTICS-DETECTION DOGS

With its smaller size, agility and extreme "play/prey" drive, the Pit Bulldog has found use as a narcotics-detection dog both in private business and in government work. Trainers rely on a dog's strong desire to play with a toy (prey item), usually a ball. The dog is taught that if it indicates the target narcotic, it will be allowed to play with its toy. Contrary to popular opinion, drug dogs are not "hooked" on the drugs, and have no desire for the drugs themselves, only for their reward. Drug work is easily taught; a dog with high "prey drive" learns to indicate the narcotics for his reward in

*Left: OTCh. Hershey, owned by Pat Cook, is a multiple high-in-trial obedience winner. **Below:** Dr. Annetta Cheek, Marilyn Brubaker-Thompson, Sharon Tatman, and B.W. Lightsey with "Puller," a SAR dog, at a training seminar.*

just a few weeks. Next the dog is taught to look in likely hiding places, such as the interiors of cars, and behind light switches in houses. The dogs can be taught to indicate in one of two ways. The first is a "passive" indication, where the dog simply sits and looks at the area where the drug is located. The other is the "active" indication, where the dog claws and tears at the area where the drug is hidden.

United States Customs and other government agencies using detection dogs have several Pit Bulls working, but due to public hysteria concerning the breed they are very careful to officially call them "crossbreeds" in many cases. It is sad indeed that many excellent working dogs have been refused by the United States Armed Forces due to this panic reaction. Dogs are picked more for appearance than working ability, and any dog that even remotely resembles a Bulldog will be refused in many cases, even if the dog has no Bulldog blood and is an excellent detection dog! Surely the narcotics- and bomb-detection programs have suffered because of this mentality.

There are a number of Bulldog and Bulldog crosses working as detection dogs for correction departments and law-enforcement agencies, and the author knows of one Pit Bulldog that works for a San Diego firm which searches fishing vessels for stowaway drugs.

The use of the Pit Bulldog in both private and government detection work is sure to increase as the outstanding drives of the dogs for this type of work are discovered. It is an outstanding area of work for this breed, showcasing its drive and determination as well as its continuing usefulness to mankind.

Hershey carting a friend.

"Petie," owned by Lyssa Noble Stoehm, works in agility, herding and obedience.

SEARCH AND RESCUE

At a recent working dog seminar held in New York state, B.W. Lightsey's Pit Bull named Puller gave an exciting demonstration of a certified SAR dog. A "lost victim" was placed in high grass at the edge of a large field. B.W. Lightsey directed Puller to search the area in a grid-like pattern. Instead of following the lost person's footsteps, Puller was running with head held high, searching for any scent that might be blowing from the "victim." Puller worked about 100 feet from B.W. and had to pass through a large group of people and dogs. The SAR dog caught a sudden scent, disappearing into the high grass. A moment later he came back into view, running up to Mr. Lightsey and giving an amazing demonstration of SAR-dog technique by leaping crossways in front of Mr. Lightsey to stop

B.W. Lightsey with Search and Rescue dog "Puller." SAR is a fantastic challenge for the versatile Pit Bull.

him. Once Mr. Lightsey stopped, he quickly led him to the victim.

B.W. and his wife have both been active in SAR for several years and both use Pit Bulls. Mrs. Lightsey's dog discovered an elderly missing person with Alzheimer's disease after a search of three days.

Anyone interested in SAR should contact local police departments for information on SAR groups which use dogs.

Many urban areas are forming Urban Disaster Rescue groups, and here the Pit Bull excels due to its moderate size and unique agility and drive. The Pit Bull can often go where a larger dog can't or won't go. Dogs which have been allowed to become aggressive toward other dogs will not be able to be used in SAR as several dogs usually work together and may be together in vehicles or planes.

For those who love the outdoors, are in shape and have a good relationship with their dog, this activity offers unique rewards.

THERAPY DOGS

The use of dogs as "therapy" in nursing homes, hospitals and convalescent centers has increased dramatically in the past few years. The APBT has always been popular for this use due to its smaller size, neat, short hair and jolly attitude. One nursing center in New Mexico even has a live-in Pit Bull which spends time with all the patients—a dog who never lacks for loving attention!

Most Pit Bulls which participate in therapy programs are family pets which spend a few hours a month visiting local nursing homes and hospitals. Acceptance of dogs in these institutions has been dramatic as staffs have realized the benefits to patients. Some owners belong to groups which stage entertaining displays of training and tricks. Others simply allow the dogs to visit one room after another, and if invited in, allow the dog to spend some time on the bed sharing a moment of affection with the resident.

Therapy Dogs International is a registering body for therapy dogs, and provides a tag, service dog card, and insurance for registered therapy dogs. A newsletter is also published periodically for members.

Any Pit Bull owner can become involved in therapy-dog

The Pit Bull excels in SAR due to its moderate size, unique agility and drive. Here Puller tugs on a pacifier.

work provided they have a calm, friendly dog which has had basic training. Elderly people are frightened by overly friendly dogs which lunge up to be petted—they prefer a quiet dog which does not force itself on them. A therapy dog must have steady nerves indeed, for many residents of convalescent centers will be unsteady, and reach out quickly and awkwardly for a dog, sometimes hitting it by accident. Others will grasp a dog and hold on tightly, and have to be literally forced to let the dog free. Very elderly people are often hard to second guess, and while most enjoy the dog's visit, some will resent or be frightened by dogs, and will resort to throwing objects at the dogs or even running them over with a wheelchair! The Pit Bulldog makes an ideal therapy dog due to its steady nerves and high pain threshold. Anyone interested in starting a visiting-dog program should contact local trainers and find out if a program is already in existence. Contact local nursing homes and explain to the program director what it is you want to do. Condition your dogs to wheelchairs, crutches and canes, and to working in close proximity with other dogs. Many homes have resident cats which must be ignored.

The therapy dog brings happiness to people who are very depressed and lonely. It is often emotionally wrenching to visit some homes, and the dogs, too, seem to become subdued after an hour in a home, as if it is wearing on them also to be so needed. Therapy work is very rewarding, and well worth the effort.

The story of "Rocky, the Therapeutic Pit Bull," written by his owner Teresa Ewing, will give you an idea of how much the Pit Bull can mean to elderly residents of nursing homes.

ROCKY, THE THERAPEUTIC PIT BULL
by Teresa Ewing

Pet therapy has long been known for bringing smiles to the

A therapy dog spends a special moment with a resident of a nursing home.

"Rocky," a registered Therapy Dog, provides comfort to an elderly woman.

unhappy, and companionship to the lonely. Dog clubs, schools and individuals with obedience-trained dogs have traveled to nursing homes and hospitals, visiting with people who have only fond memories of the dogs with whom they once shared their lives. The value of friendly, obedient dogs as therapy for troubled children, heart patients and the elderly is documented repeatedly in current studies.

About four years ago I had entered two of my American Pit Bull Terriers in an obedience trial in Cheyenne, Wyoming. There I met Ann and Jack Butrick, who are very active in pet therapy. After getting lavish kisses from Rocky they encouraged me to get involved in pet therapy. I had often wanted to do this but felt I would be rejected with my Pit Bulls. Today, with the support and encouragement of Jack and Ann, I now have seven of my eight Pit

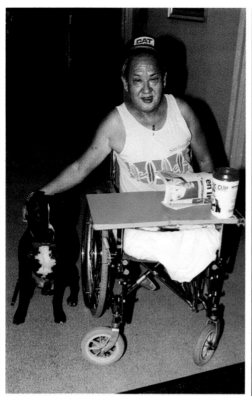

Timberline's Rocky, U-CD and a friend at the Westland Manor, where he was named "Volunteer of the Year" for two years.

Bulls registered with Therapy Dogs International, and am very active in pet therapy. I am very active in obedience and I also do public relations work every chance I get. It has not been easy getting accepted in therapy work with this breed. I try to forget how many places said "NO!" as soon as I said American Pit Bull Terrier. Well, being just as stubborn as my dogs, I continued to make call after call. Once given a chance I knew I could make a difference. After all, I had once had to get accepted in obedience and that was not easy either. Now my dogs and I are very wanted in

many situations from therapy work to educational showcases. We always leave a good impression.

In doing therapy work we visit hospitals, nursing homes and hospice centers. Our favorite is nursing homes, as most of the residents are there for the rest of their lives and get very few visitors. They seem to benefit the most by a visit from a wagging tail. I really enjoy doing one-on-one visits with the residents in their rooms. I use certain dogs for certain types of visits. Maggie visits head injury patients as she is a quiet, gentle girl. These patients need a softer-type visit. There is not much talking on these visits, so Maggie just gets to relax with the patients while they pet her.

Shorty did specialty work with cancer patients at the hospices as he was one himself. One of his lungs had to be removed due to cancer. Hospice patients took great hope and strength from seeing how well and quickly he had recovered. Some patients even compared surgery scars with him! Some told Shorty their problems. He knew that they needed to talk and to touch. Others would visit for hours and never say a thing—but the love was there and you knew it. Shorty was there for them when they had no hope left. This is probably the hardest type of visit. It became harder still when cancer returned to Shorty's other lung. He continued to make visits while undergoing chemotherapy. This gave him still another closeness with the patients. The visits became increasingly difficult, and Shorty gave us an example of the "heart" this breed is known for. Shorty was that special dog we are all looking for. He touched many hearts in his lifetime, and he still lives on in his children.

Rocky is my clown. He brings smiles to the lonely residents of nursing homes. Many residents are reminded of Pit Bulls they owned in their youth when they see Rocky's antics. When Rocky feels he has stayed too long visiting a resident, he will pick up his own leash and walk out of the room on to his next friend. Rocky has been honored twice by being named "Volunteer of the Year" at one home we visit. He has even been honored with a party.

Breed-specific laws have made it difficult for owner Teresa Ewing to continue Rocky's loving care.

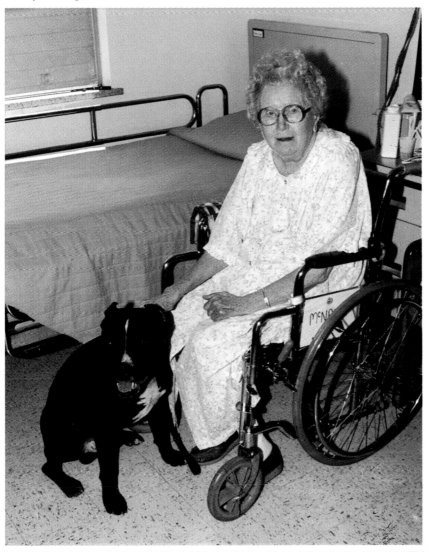

*Bandog Thriller, TDI, HC, representing
Therapy Dogs International at a mall.*

and AKC trials, which means
they scored higher than any of
the other dogs (of all breeds) at
the show. In an AKC show this
can mean outscoring over a
hundred dogs at a show. Dogs
which have earned this
distinction include: Scotswood
Sun Bear, Bandog Dread, Fraja
Earth Shaker, China White, and
Ledge Rocks Blue Velvet—to
name but a few.

OTCh. Scotswood Sun Beam,
UD, was the first of any "bull
and/or bull and terrier" breed to
earn the title of Obedience Trial
Champion (OTCh.). Hershey, as
she was called, was a little black
Bulldog found wandering the
streets of East Oakland,
California, untrained, unloved
and covered in fleas. Taken in by
renowned trainer Pat Cook, she
completed her AKC CD title in

three shows, earning a Dog
World award by scoring 195 (out
of 200) or better each time
shown. While she was not AKC-
registered, she was shown by
means of an Individual Listing
Privilege (ILP) which allows
purebred but unregistered dogs
to compete in obedience trials.
The AKC has since stopped
issuing ILPs to any dog which
could not prove it was of
"American Staffordshire"
bloodlines instead of UKC
bloodlines, a sad and foolish
mistake since two of the breed's
biggest winners have most
definitely not been of Staff
blood.

At the Gaines Western
Regional Dog Obedience
Championships in Las Vegas,
1983, Hershey placed in the
Open division—another first for

*Teresa Ewing, who owns seven famous
Therapy Dogs, visiting with Bandog Brittania
and Bandog Dread.*

the breed. Hershey was the top Am. Staff in obedience rankings for five consecutive years, and often also in the Terrier Group as a whole. On May 14, 1987, Hershey became the first ever American Staffordshire/Pit registered. Both the AKC and the UKC hold sanctioned obedience trials. Unregistered dogs can be shown at "fun matches" which are held all over the U.S. To find a listing of fun matches, contact your local kennel club.

Teresa Ewing's family of obedience- and Therapy Dog-titled Pit Bulls. They are products of Mason-Tudor-Spartan breeding.

Bulldog AKC Obedience Trial Champion! Hershey has gone high in trial at the prestigious Malibu Kennel Club and also the large Golden Gate Kennel Club. Not bad for a "street kid"!

Anyone interested in obedience competition with their Bulldog should contact the registry with which their dog is

TRACKING DOGS

The sport of teaching dogs to follow human scent is both fun and practical. Tracking differs from search and rescue in that the dog follows the actual footsteps of the person instead of searching the wind for a tell-tale scent. Tracking takes great determination and concentration, and a well-trained tracking dog displays a tenacity and grit unrivaled in many other dog sports.

Tracking is exhausting for a dog, and many competition tracks are a mile or longer and often through rough terrain.

Dogs are trained to track by having the owner drop small pieces of food on their trail as they walk, and leaving a larger reward at the end of the trail. The trail is very short to start—sometimes no longer than 20 feet. The dog is encouraged to keep its head low, and to sniff carefully. The dog is also taught to indicate any article, such as wallet or gun, dropped by the person they are tracking.

The AKC and Schutzhund clubs offer tracking tests, and the Pit Bulldog has often distinguished himself in this field. It is a credit to his "all-purpose" history that he retains a good nose. One great tracking AmStaff, Finale, owned by Marilyn Brubaker Thompson, was renowned for his tracking

Hershey, the famous obedience Pit Bull, looks over a litter of Border Collie pups.

Above: "Morgan," a very special Therapy Dog owned by Teresa Ewing. **Below right:** Dr. Rudy Kasni APBT, "Petie," a personal protection dog.

abilities, and held records to impress any Bloodhound. Several times Finale scored a perfect 100 points on the most complex of Schutzhund tracking tests. Marilyn and Finale even went to Germany where her Pit Bull outscored Germany's best German Shepherds to earn highest scoring tracking dog at a Schutzhund trial! Perhaps Finale's greatest performance was completing a near perfect FH track (Marilyn lost a few points by a handler error) days before he died of cancer. A game little dog that worked for his beloved owner to the best of his great ability in the hot Florida sun, Finale enjoyed a career as a tracking dog

Two Pit Bulls owned by the Peterson family of Ohio. Both dogs are very well obedience-trained.

that stands as a testimony to the breed's great gameness.

HUNTING DOGS

Some people use Pit Bulldogs to hunt wild hogs and other large game. This "sport" is practiced primarily in Hawaii, northern California and in the southern states. Bulldogs used for this purpose are generally large. This use, very similar to the breed's original purpose, is practiced by very few people as it results in severe damage and death to many good dogs. A wild hog has savage tusks and will stand and fight. It seems a shame that the hogs and the dogs have to be injured and killed for man's "sport."

A few Pit Bulls have been trained as bird dogs, and have been used to good effect. The breed possesses a strong prey drive, and some are even natural pointers, freezing in position when they come across a bird. Pit Bulldogs make exceptional retrievers, and do well in retriever-type trials when given the opportunity.

The great Cheek's Red Baroness, SchH III, U-UD has proudly represented the breed in national Schutzhund competition. Owner, Annetta Cheek.

Above: *Pat Cook's famous OTCH. Scottwoods' Sunbeam Hershey.* ***Right:*** *Any object can be placed on a dog walk to make it more difficult, such as a tire.*

The Bulldog at Play

Uniquely strong drives coupled with a strong, agile body and a happy, willing nature make the Pit Bull, without doubt, one of the top competition training dogs available today. Because many Bulldog owners traditionally kept more dogs than they could train and care for and kept their dogs outside on chains, away from human interaction, many people came to believe they were an

Lyssa Noble-Stoehm and "Tiggy" show perfect heeling form. Lyssa uses all motivational training with no force.

unintelligent breed fit only to live their lives on a chain. Even many owners of APBT would state that they did not find their dogs to be very intelligent. Little wonder when one saw how the dogs were kept! Any dog chained in a back yard and rarely played or worked with will develop into as dull and unintelligent a creature as the owner who imprisons it!

In reality, the Pit Bull is as smart as any dog, and coupled with an incredibly strong desire to please its owner, is capable of learning the most complex obedience and other training tasks. Because it is a happy dog, filled with "play drives" which, when used properly, make training more of a game than a form of discipline, training the APBT can be as much fun as playing with him. The following sports are ones in which the Pit Bull has already distinguished himself as a top competitor. With a Bulldog, no training title is beyond reach.

UKC OBEDIENCE

The United Kennel Club offers obedience titles for all registered APBTs. There are three titles, representing three levels of difficulty. The first level (Novice) is obtainable by the novice trainer after a standard eight-week obedience course, if the dog is trained diligently. The second level (Open) is quite challenging, and represents a dog that is highly trained. The third level (Utility), rarely reached, takes years of training and practice to attain, and represents a worthy goal indeed.

United Companion Dog (U-CD)

HEELING ON LEAD: In this exercise the dog must demonstrate its ability to stay in "heel position" (head and shoulders next to handler's left knee) with a lead on but hanging loose. The handler will maneuver about the ring following the judge's instructions to walk "normal, slow, fast," and to make right, left and about turns. The judge will also instruct the handler to stop several times during the heeling pattern, at which time the dog must sit in the heel position without a command to do so. The handler may give only one command to the dog, to heel, each time the judge tells the handler to begin heeling again. While heeling, the team is passed twice by a steward (helper) walking in close proximity.

After the handler and dog team have executed their heeling pattern, the judge will ask two stewards to come into the ring and take up positions about eight feet apart facing each other. The dog and handler team must then heel around these two posts in a figure-eight form, stopping twice to sit.

HEELING OFF LEAD: The team then repeats the heeling exercises with the leash taken off, and the dog free beside the handler.

STAND FOR EXAMINATION: Now the dog (off lead for the rest of the exercises) is placed into a comfortable standing position and told to stay. The handler stands about six feet away while the judge approaches the dog and does an examination of the dog by touching it on the head, neck and body. The judge then steps back and tells the handler to return to the dog. The handler returns around behind the dog and assumes the heel position, and the exercise is finished. The dog cannot move (more than minor movement of a foot) in order to pass.

RECALL: The dog is placed in the sitting position about ten feet

Lyssa with Ch. Big Time's Grease Lightning, CGC shows good on-lead heeling form.

A happy work/sport dog in perfect heel position. The dog is attentive and joyful.

from a jump which is equal to the dog's height at the shoulder or two feet, whichever is less. The dog is told to stay and the handler walks around the jump to a point approximately ten feet away from the jump facing the dog. At the judge's signal the handler calls the dog and the dog must come in a straight line (jumping over the jump) and come to sit in front of the handler. The handler is allowed only one command which may include the dog's name first, for example: "Rex, come!" At the judge's command the handler tells the dog to return to heel position, and the dog must do so by either walking around behind the handler and coming up to heel on the left side, or by swinging its rear end around on the left side of

the handler and thereby moving in a half circle to return to heel position.

SIT-STAY: When a dog is done with the individual exercises, a group of dogs from the same level will return to the ring together to perform the group exercise. The dogs will line up in the order which they were shown in, and will all line up in a row on the far side of the ring. The leashes will be removed and the dogs must sit quietly beside their handlers. The dogs are about 18 inches apart, and the dogs may not sniff each other. At the judge's signal, the handlers will all leave the dogs and cross the ring. The handlers will turn to face their dogs for the full one minute that the dogs maintain their sitting position. The handler may not speak to or motion to the dog. After a minute

The signal to stand is given.

the judge will order the handlers back to their dogs, and the handlers will return around behind their dog and resume the heel position. At the judge's command, "Exercise finished," the dogs may be released from their sit command.

HONOR EXERCISE: Either before or after a team does its individual exercises, a team will be required to perform the honor exercise. The dog is made to lie down in a corner of the ring away from the direct path of the dog to work next. While the other dog is heeling, the honoring dog must remain lying down, with its handler across the ring from it. The honoring dog must not stand up, move or interfere with the working dog. When the working dog is finished heeling, the judge will order the honoring dog's handler to return to their dog, and the exercise is finished.

United Companion Dog Excellent (U-CDX)

HEELING OFF-LEAD: The team enters the ring off-lead, and

The signal to come.

proceeds to do a heeling pattern directed by the judge similar to the same exercise in the Novice class. The team will then do a figure-eight heeling pattern around the two stewards.

RETRIEVE ON FLAT: With the dog sitting in heel position (all exercises in Open are performed with the leash off), the handler tells the dog to stay and then throws a dumbbell (wooden

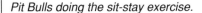

Pit Bulls doing the sit-stay exercise.

retrieving object shaped like a miniature weight-lifting dumbbell) about 20 feet in front of the dog. The dog must remain in heel position until the judge directs the handler to command the dog to retrieve, and the handler has so commanded. The dog should move out briskly, pick up the object and return quickly to sit before the handler, presenting the dumbbell. At the judge's

which form a barrier twice the length of the height the dog was required to jump over for the retrieve over a jump. The handler leaves the dog and stands beside the jump. At the judge's order, the handler commands the dog to jump directly over the obstacle. Without an additional command, the dog will turn as soon as it lands and come to the handler and sit straight in front. At the

Four Pit Bulldogs doing a group down-stay. A gaggle of geese wander near the group.

command the handler takes the dumbbell from the dog and orders the dog back into heel position.

RETRIEVE OVER A JUMP: The retrieve on flat exercise is repeated with the addition of a jump (the same height as the dog jumped in Novice) over which the handler throws the dumbbell. The dog must clear the jump both going for and returning with the dumbbell.

BROAD JUMP: The dog is positioned about eight feet in front of a series of low hurdles

judge's command, the handler commands the dog to return to heel position.

DROP ON RECALL: The team performs the same exercise as the novice "recall," except that when the dog has come halfway across the ring towards the handler the handler shall command/signal the dog to drop in its tracks, and the dog shall remain there while a steward walks by in close proximity. After the steward has passed the judge shall order the handler to

A Pit Bull returns to present dumbbell during a retrieve exercise.

United Utility Dog (U-UD)

SIGNAL EXERCISE: This is similar to the heeling exercise in Open, except the dog is commanded to heel with only a hand signal and no vocal cues. After the dog has performed a heeling pattern, the judge will command the handler to stop. When the handler stops he signals the dog to remain standing. At another command from the judge the handler crosses the ring and turns to face the dog. On the judge's signal, the handler signals the dog to drop, then to sit, then to come. After the dog has sat in front, the handler signals the dog to return to heel position. During this entire exercise the handler may not speak to the dog.

ARTICLES: Next the handler presents six identical metal articles to the judge who places them out in a random pattern in the ring. These articles are

command the dog to return to the handler. After sitting directly in front of the handler, the dog will then be commanded to return to heel position.

LONG SIT: This exercise is performed the same way as the long sit in the Novice class except that the handlers leave the ring and are out of the dog's sight for five minutes.

HONORING: The same as in Novice, except that the handler is out of the ring and out of the dog's sight while it is honoring.

In Schutzhund obedience the dog must return with dumbbell over a 39-inch jump.

sterilized, and do not bear the dog owner's scent. The judge selects one article and hands it to the handler who rubs it momentarily to impact his scent on it. The judge places the scented article among the unscented ones. The dog is then turned to face the articles and ordered to seek out the scented one. The dog must move quickly out to the articles, scent them, and select the correct articles, retrieving it to the owner and sitting in front. The handler takes the article from the dog and orders the dog back to heel position.

DROP ON RECALL: Same as in Open.

STRAIGHT RECALL: Same as in Novice (no jump).

Above: *Petie selects the correct utility scent article.* **Below:** *Petie returns with the article.*

An APBT leaping over the high jump used in open and utility classes.

GLOVE RETRIEVE: With the dog and handler sitting at the six o'clock position, three white cotton work gloves are placed at the nine o'clock, 12 o'clock and three o'clock positions across the ring from the dog. The judge indicates which glove the dog is to retrieve and the handler directs the dog to that glove. The dog must retrieve only the glove indicated.

DIRECTED GLOVE RETRIEVE: The glove-retrieve exercise is repeated, only the dog is sent directly out toward the 12 o'clock position. As the dog nears that glove, the handler

Here an APBT flies over the broad jump, as required in open obedience classes.

commands the dog to sit. After the dog has sat, the judge will tell the handler which glove the dog is to retrieve. Now the handler must redirect the dog, either to the two side gloves or straight back toward the glove the dog was headed for. The dog must retrieve the correct glove.

DIRECTED JUMPING: Now two jumps are brought into the ring and placed roughly in the nine o'clock and three o'clock positions relative to team. At the judge's order the dog is sent straight back to the 12 o'clock position and stopped near the edge of the ring. The judge then indicates either the solid jump (used in Novice and Open) or the bar jump (a jump that is only a bar placed on two uprights at the same height as the solid jump). The dog must take its direction from its owner's signal and command, and return to the owner by deviating over the directed jump. The dog is then ordered to return to heel and the exercise is repeated, with the dog performing the jump it did not do during the first portion of the exercises.

Further information on United Kennel Club obedience can be obtained by writing: United Kennel Club Obedience Dept., 100 E. Kilgore Rd., Kalamazoo, MI 49001-5598

AMERICAN KENNEL CLUB

The AKC offers obedience titles for dogs registered as American Staffordshire Terriers, and for any dog with an "ILP" number which indicates that the dog is a purebred but unregistered Am. Staff. Because of the AKC's policy of denying that the Am. Staff is simply an APBT registered with a different registry, the AKC will not willingly give out ILP numbers to purebred APBTs. APBTs of unknown history have a better chance of being recognized by the AKC as purebred then do well-bred APBTs whose ancestors have been registered with a different registry!

"ILP" stands for Individual Listing Privilege. The ILP is obtained by requesting an ILP form from the AKC and then submitting it with color photos of your dog. The form asks you to state why and how you think your dog is a purebred (Am. Staff). Many APBTs have been dogs which are/were AKC-registered, and it is a good idea to point this out. All dogs are required to be altered (spayed or neutered) in

Here the owner goes around the jump and calls the dog.

order to receive an ILP, which only grants the owner the right to show the dog in AKC obedience trials and tracking titles. Most of the "Am. Staffs" which have won "highest scoring dog in trial" at AKC obedience trials have been APBTs registered with the AKC with an ILP number.

Like the UKC, the AKC offers classes in Novice, Open and Utility. In fact the classes are more similar than they are different. The AKC classes will be listed here with only the difference between AKC and UKC pointed out.

COMPANION DOG

HEELING ON LEAD: Same as UKC except no stewards will be walking in the ring while the dog is working and no honoring dog will be present.

The signal to return to the heel position.

HEELING OFF-LEAD: Same as UKC.

STAND FOR EXAM: Same as UKC.

In UKC obedience the dog must return to its owner over a low jump.

The signal to sit up from a down.

RECALL: Exercise is the same except the dog is not required to jump.

LONG SIT: Same as UKC.

LONG DOWN: Same as the long sit except the dog lies down and remains down with the handler across the ring for three minutes.

Companion Dog Excellent (CDX)

HEEL OFF LEAD: Same as UKC except no steward in the ring.

RETRIEVE ON FLAT: Same as UKC.

RETRIEVE OVER JUMP: Same as UKC except jump is slightly higher (one and a quarter times the dog's height at the shoulders).

DROP ON RECALL: Same as UKC except no steward will walk past the dog.

BROAD JUMP: Same as UKC except jump is two and one-half times the dog's height at the shoulder.

LONG SIT: Same as in novice except the handlers are out of the dog's sight for three minutes.

LONG DOWN: Same as the long sit except the handlers are out of the dog's sight for five minutes.

Utility Dog (UD)

SIGNAL EXERCISE: Same as UKC,

ARTICLES: Same as UKC except the dog must indicate first a metal article, then a leather article that has been touched by the handler.

Hershey doing the utility scent discrimination exercise.

DIRECTED RETRIEVE: Same as the first-glove exercise in UKC. The dog is turned toward the correct glove and scnt directly toward it.

STAND IN MOTION: While heeling, the dog is commanded to stand, and must remain standing while the handler proceeds away from the dog. At the end of the ring the handler turns and faces the dog. The judge will approach the dog and examine the dog by touching it on the body and head. At the judge's signal the handler will command the dog to return and go directly to the heel position.

DIRECTED JUMPING: Same as UKC.

TRACKING

The sport of tracking is a quiet, peaceful pastime, excellent for persons who live in isolated or very rural areas. The goals of tracking tests are to test the dog's training and ability to follow the exact trail left by a person, and to indicate any objects dropped by that person along the track. Tracking tests vary in difficulty, and only the FH title offered by Schutzhund clubs is available at this time to all APBTs (registered or not). The FH is the most difficult test, but well worth the time and effort required to bring a dog to that level of training.

AKC Tracking Titles

The AKC offers tracking tests for all American Staffordshire Terriers and all APBTs ILP'd as Am. Staffs. The tests are described below:

Tracking Dog (TD)

To enter a Tracking Dog test, a dog must be over six months of age and must have been certified by an AKC tracking judge to be competent to enter the test. This certification is required because AKC tracking tests are rare and entry is difficult to gain. Therefore only qualified dogs are desired.

A TD test is always run on grass, and the terrain is consistent. The track is approximately 800 yards long. The dog is given two starting flags, 30 yards apart, which point out the direction of the first part of the track. The track is laid by a tracklayer, then aged about one-half hour. The dog and handler approach the start, and the dog is shown the start of the track. If the dog becomes confused, it can be restarted so long as it has not passed the second flag, 30 yards from the start. In a TD test, the dog must be wearing a harness, and may be on a line which is from 20 to 40 feet in length. The dog may urinate and defecate while on the track, and may wander off the track as far as the 40-foot line allows. As long as the dog follows the general direction of the track, and the object is found by the handler, the dog will pass.

Because a certain amount of latitude is given to dogs in AKC

Diane Jessup and Bandog Dread near the start of an AKC Tracking Dog track. Dread earned his TD on the first try.

tests, some dogs which are barely tracking have been titled. On the other hand, some very good dogs have run some very good tracks, and these titles are worthy indeed.

Tracking Dog Excellent (TDX)

Any dog which has earned a TD title may enter a TDX test. This is a much more difficult test, and the dog must follow a trail approximately 1200 yards long and aged over three hours. This track will have been confused by the passage of two other persons walking across the path of the tracklayer. The dog must still wear a harness and 20- to 40-foot line. The dog is given a single starting stake, at which an article is lying. The dog must ascertain the direction of the track and must indicate three other articles placed along and at the end of the track.

This dog has dropped on recall as it was coming to its owner. The dog is told to "down" as it runs in toward the owner.

The TDX is a worthy title indeed, and a dog must have a certain level of proficiency to obtain it. It should be remembered that the method of tracking used in tests is quite different from that used in search and rescue. In search and rescue (SAR) work the dogs "airscent," or follow the airborne scent of a person, more than the odor of the crushed ground where the person has trod, which is what the best of the tracking dogs do. The SAR dog ranges about attempting to locate the airborne scent of a person, not following the exact trail of where the person may have walked.

Schutzhund Tracking Titles
  FH—Tracking Dog
  All APBTs, purebred or of uncertain ancestry, registered or unregistered, may compete for the premier tracking title, the German FH. In order to enter a trial, a dog must be registered with the Independent Work and Sport Dog Association, an American Schutzhund organization. Once the dog is registered and has a scorebook, the dog may be entered in the FH as many times as desired. Unlike AKC tracking, Schutzhund tracking is scored, so that even should a person pass the FH on the first attempt, he can continue to enter in an

attempt to reach the perfect score of 100 points.

The FH is about 1200 yards long, aged three hours, and goes over changes in terrain (grass to dirt, etc.). This track is also fouled by another person walking over the path of the tracklayer in several places. The dog is given a single starting flag and must ascertain the direction of travel of the tracklayer. When indicating the several dropped articles along the tracklayer's path, the dog must indicate them by either lying down, sitting or standing near them, or retrieving it to the handler. It must do the same indication for all articles. While tracking, the dog may wear a harness or a plain choke collar to which a 30-foot line is attached.

Unlike AKC tracking, the Schutzhund track is much more disciplined, and the dog is not allowed to wander off the track to any great extent. Ideally the dog will follow footstep to footstep, and each time the dog leaves this ideal position points will be deducted. Even when the wind is blowing, the area where the tracklayer has walked will hold the scent of the crushed vegetation or soil and will be the truest track. Points are also deducted for a dog that urinates or defecates while working, and for handler errors.

HOW TO TRAIN A DOG TO TRACK

There are several excellent books available to help the novice dog trainer begin tracking with his dog. If possible, visit a local Schutzhund club and observe tracking sessions. There are as many methods of tracking training as there are trainers, and you must find one with whom you are comfortable. Most trainers use a motivational

Bandog Dread begins the track where he earned his International Police Dog title, level III.

Annetta Cheek's wonderful working bitch PR Cheek's Baroness, SchH III, FH, U-UD shows winning tracking form.

method, based on the dog's desire to eat. Small tracks are laid which are baited with food and the hungry dog is encouraged to follow the track in order to eat. Some trainers believe you must force a dog to track, and train their dogs through physical pain. Top tracking trainers such as Marilyn Brubaker Thompson, who has scored numerous perfect 100 scores on the German FH title, do not believe in the force method, and use only food and praise with perfect results.

A dog may begin tracking training as young as eight weeks of age—the earlier the better. To begin tracking training, you will need a plain leather collar, a six-foot lead, a small leather article such as an old wallet, a starting stake (any stick with a piece of surveyor's tape tied to the top) and a portion of some food the dog particularly likes. The time of day that you track is unimportant—just remember that very hot, dry days make for very difficult tracking conditions and are not too desirable for starting a new dog. Traditionally early morning, while there is still dew on the ground, has been considered the best.

Locate an area that is relatively untraveled. You do not want confusing cross tracks at this point in your training! To start you want nice even grass about one to three inches high. If the grass is much higher a puppy will have to struggle too much and an older dog will not

This solid Colby-bred bitch is titled in Schutzhund, weight-pulling , herding, and obedience. Another example of the breed's versatility.

"Angel" finds that sunglasses help her track.

will scent the first food article and its head will drop. While the dog is actually sniffing the ground, allow it to go forward *at a walking pace.* Do not let the dog run or it will become inaccurate and sloppy. As the dog finds pieces of food, allow it to stop and eat, praising it quietly. If you are too loud with your praise you will distract the dog. When it has finished eating, hold it in place until it drops its nose again, then proceed forward. The dog must not learn that it can simply walk forward hoping to find food. It must learn that it must be actually *tracking* in order to move forward.

When you reach the end of the track, show the dog the article, praise it wildly and allow it to eat its food. When it is done eating take the dog away from the track the opposite way that you left the track. Do not allow it to continue tracking once it has finished the track.

With a beginning dog, attempt two such tracks each session, once or twice a week is sufficient. Be sure the dog has not eaten for at least a few hours before tracking, longer for the older dogs. Do not deprive a dog of food longer than 24 hours for tracking purposes. If the dog will not track, try a different bait food. Remember, tracking is a sport, and the dog should not suffer for it. Most dogs will track willingly if slightly hungry. Most dogs that will not track for food have either had a bad experience with a force tracker or they are so overfed at home that they have no desire to go looking through grass for food.

As training progresses, the elements of training stay the same. The dog may only move forward when it is actually scenting the ground. Gradually as the dog becomes track sure, you may move back to the end of the six-foot lead. If the dog begins to wander more than a few inches off the direct path, quickly go back up on the lead and hold the dog back to the track for a while. When you reach the article at the end of the track, or any you may place along the way, begin gently pushing the dog into a down or sit position and then praising and feeding it. This way the dog quickly learns that it must lie down or sit before being rewarded for finding an article. After months of training, when the dog comes across an article and does not drop or sit quickly, a slight correction with the lead may be used to remind it.

It takes about six months of diligent training to prepare a dog for a TD or SchH I-level tracking test. The use of the long line is unimportant in training, but should be practiced a few times before a trial to accustom the dog to seeing you so far behind him. Also, have another person lay the track (and use an article unfamiliar to the dog) several times before a test. Most dogs have no problem changing from tracking one person to another, but it is a good idea to familiarize the dog with the practice.

As the dog becomes proficient, begin lengthening the time the track is aged, and begin walking into changes of terrain. Always approach each new difficulty with a six-foot lead, to help the dog

Gr. Ch. Tyee's Boy Bosworth owned by Joyce Klahn.

UKC/AKC Ch. Rowdytown Stormy Weather, U-CD, TT owned by Renee Frendenburg.

stay on the track. It is a natural tendency for a dog to cast about wildly when reaching a difficult portion, when actually the dog need only work harder at staying on the track he is on. That is what you must help him understand.

Tracking is a low-stress, natural, enjoyable sport, and is overlooked by many who could benefit from the exercise and relaxation. What could be more enjoyable than spending a little time along with your best friend out in the country?

SCHUTZHUND

Schutzhund is a German word meaning "guardian dog." The Schutzhund trial was developed first as a testing ground for guard and defense-type dogs, not only to test an individual dog's level of training but also to evaluate dogs for breeding purposes. Only dogs with sufficient working drives could pass, and therefore these dogs were suitable for breeding. In Europe to this day, dogs of guard and defense breeds are required to earn a Schutzhund I title before being used for breeding.

Schutzhund is a stylized police K-9 trial. The dogs are required to perform all the tasks a police dog would be required to do, such as tracking a human, complex obedience and searching for, apprehension and guarding of a suspect. Today Schutzhund is primarily a sport, and the dogs are trained with this in mind. For safety purposes, many dogs are trained to be extremely "clean," that is, they are trained in such a way that they are less likely to bite a human outside of a trial situation. A dog can be trained to be a good, tough Schutzhund dog and still not be considered an "attack dog." The goal in Schutzhund is to produce a well-rounded canine, a dog which displays all the drives and training necessary to perform police work. The goal is not necessarily to produce dogs which are ready to "go to work" on the street as a police K-9 without additional training. Because it is a sport, it is stylized, and therefore not completely practical.

Al Banuelos works a red/red-nose in Schutzhund training.

John Tatman with Tatman's Samson, ACE, SchH III, one of the first Pit Bulls to compete in Schutzhund on a national level.

For instance, the dogs are taught to withstand a few sharp blows with a stick while they are fighting the suspect. This is to show that the dogs possess the courage and toughness to withstand physical intimidation from a human. In real police work, a dog should be taught to release its grip and bite the arm that is hitting them—in order for the dog to avoid injury. In Schutzhund, the dog maintains its grip to show courage—not necessarily practical training, but making temperament assessment easier.

On the other hand, one should never assume that a dog titled in the sport of Schutzhund is not capable of practical police or defense work—they are highly trained, and generally of a very capable temperament. Many Schutzhund-trained dogs have become police dogs with no additional training.

More than any other sport, Schutzhund demands dedication from its enthusiasts. It is the only dog sport where the dog must master three separate skills. On trial day, the dog must perform more than a complex defense portion. The Schutzhund trainer must have

Bandog Dread holds Mike Duncan in the blind during Schutzhund work.

the time and discipline to train in all three portions equally. And whereas an obedience enthusiast can get up every morning and go out and practice obedience, or the weight-pull person can practice weight pull, the Schutzhund trainer must always decide, "This morning should it be tracking, obedience, or bite work?" And because the training is so extensive, a good trainer always schedules regular time slots where the dog is just allowed to goof off and be a dog.

Anyone considering the sport of Schutzhund must think long and hard about the entire commitment required. Many people become fascinated with the complex bite work, yet will not put in the time required for tracking and obedience. Most clubs realize this, and put strict

requirements on members to attend all three training phases. The best clubs will not allow a member to participate in the bite work training unless they have been present for all phases on a given day. This method quickly weeds out those who are seeking only a dog trained in guard work. Beware of clubs, though, which do not insist on obedience training *before* bite training. Some clubs feel that training a dog in obedience before it has developed a strong bite will ruin the dog. This may be true of soft dogs, but a true Bulldog will develop much better if he receives a well-rounded curriculum of obedience and beginning bite work at the same time. A good dog can withstand practical training—if your dog is too soft to handle obedience and bite work at the same time, then it has no business in Schutzhund training.

Another consideration is the scarcity of good clubs. There are two main organizations which sanction Schutzhund trials in the U.S. One is United Schutzhund Clubs of America, a club formed by German Shepherd breeders, and while at this date they still allow certain other breeds to compete, they do not have a "may the best dog win" attitude, and bar any breed but Shepherds from competing at a top level. In the '80s, the vice-president of the national club sent out a memo to all clubs asking them to not allow APBTs to train in their clubs for fear that the panic associated with them would somehow draw attention to the fact that German Shepherds were being trained "to bite" in Schutzhund clubs. This was a very unfortunate act, and resulted in some very good APBTs not being allowed to compete before the public, where their control, obedience and friendliness had always impressed spectators favorably.

The other national club is the German-based DVG, which has its roots in the German sport dog club. DVG trials were traditionally open to all breeds. In 1992 Pit Bulls as well as several other mastiff-type breeds were suddenly, and with no explanation, given score cards which stated they could not enter Schutzhund trials. There was much protest and confusion, and it appears that it may have been an attempt to keep a few top Bulldogs from competing on a national level. At the time of this writing, it is unclear if all breeds may compete or not, and if not why.

Laura Lightsey's APBT learning to guard the "suspect" for Schutzhund trials.

The well-known Tatman's Samson, ACE, SchH III, doing a perfect hold and bark at a Schutzhund trial.

Whatever the reason, irreparable damage has been done to the DVG organization.

Unfair prejudice still exists in both organizations. In United Schutzhund Clubs of America trials and newsletters a pit bull must be called an "American Staffordshire," regardless of whether it is one or not. This prevents many good Bulldog people from competing in this club. In DVG it is possible to get a scorecard with APBT on it, but it is sometimes still a struggle.

Schutzhund One (SchH I)

The SchH I title is often considered a beginning title by those familiar with the sport. Actually, in earning a SchH I title a dog does everything it will have to do to obtain a SchH III title, the only difference being that at each level the routines become slightly more difficult. For instance, the elements of tracking are the same regardless of the title, the distance and degree of difficulty are just greater for the higher degrees. A SchH I title is a great accomplishment for any dog and handler, and represents a tremendous amount of commitments.

SchH I TRACKING: The track is laid by the dog's own handler, and generally wallet-sized pieces of leather. The dog must follow the track accurately (not wandering off several feet to the side) and indicate the articles as it finds them by stopping and either

Bandog Dread performing at the Canine Aggression Research Center. Dread travelled all over the U.S., Canada, and Caribbean helping officers realize that Pit Bulls are only as dangerous as their owners.

is 300 to 400 paces long. It contains two articles (one in the middle of the second leg, one at the end) and is aged at least 20 minutes. The dog may be tracked on a 30-foot lead or may be off-lead. The track must have two right-angle turns. The articles are standing, sitting or lying down by the article. Dogs may also retrieve the article to their handlers. Points will be deducted for a dog which works sloppily, urinates while working, or fails to indicate an article. Points will also be deducted for handler errors.

Spartagus with agitator Dave Houchins.

Gr. Ch. Panda's Gallant Spartagus, TD, CD, SchHII, VB, AD, U-CD with Schutzhund agitator Darrel Hall. In Schutzhund the stick seen in Darrel's hand is used to test the dog's courage.

The author puts the finishing touches on Gr. Ch. Beringer's Schutzhund training. Beringer shows perfect find and bark form.

SchH I OBEDIENCE: The dog must heel on lead, heel off lead, heel through a group. The dog will be tested for gunshyness while heeling off lead. The dog will then perform the "in motion" exercises, which include sitting and lying down on command while heeling. The handler may not stop or look back at the dog after commanding it to sit or drop. The dog performs a recall from about 40 yards from where it was dropped in motion.

The dog then retrieves an article (generally a dumbbell) on the flat, and then goes over a 39-inch jump. Then the dog is commanded to "Go out," directly away from its owner in a straight line until told to stop. The distance is about 40 yards. To complete the obedience phase a dog must do a down stay exercise while the handler is 30 paces away with their back turned. The dog will perform this exercise on the field while another dog is working.

SchH I PROTECTION: The dog is brought on the field and sent to search two blinds. The helper is hiding in the second blind to be searched. The dog must search under control. Upon finding the helper the dog must hold the helper in place by barking, and may not leave the helper at all. The dog may not bite the helper. The handler comes and gets control of the dog and the helper goes to the other blind and hides. Now the handler heels toward where the helper is hiding.The helper attacks the handler from behind the blind, and the dog must grasp the helper firmly without command. The helper will hit the dog twice with a padded stick to test the dog's courage. The helper then gives up and the dog is commanded to release. The dog then stays guarding the helper while the handler searches the helper. The handler then returns to the dog and grasps him by the collar. Now the helper will run away making threatening gestures and noises. When the helper has gone about 50 paces the dog is released. The helper turns toward and charges the dog, making exaggerated threatening motions. The dog must hit hard, grasping firmly, and when the helper stops moving must release on command. The dog must remain guarding the suspect until the handler arrives and again searches the suspect. Then the handler and dog escort the suspect to the judge.

Schutzhund Two (SchH II)

SchH II TRACKING: The track will be laid by a stranger and be 400 to 500 paces long, and aged at least 30 minutes. There will be two articles and two right-angle turns.

SchH II OBEDIENCE: Similar to SchH I obedience with the following additions: the dog now retrieves a 2-pound dumbbell on the flat, a 1½-pound dumbbell over the 39-inch jump, and must retrieve over a six-foot wall.

SchH II PROTECTION: The dog must now search all six blinds on the field, as directed by the handler. The dog will hold the suspect in the blind by barking. When the handler arrives the dog is called back into heel position and the suspect steps out. The dog guards the suspect as the handler searches them.

Laura Lightsey's APBT takes a firm grip. This dog is also a certified SAR dog with a find to her credit.

Ch. Spartan's Zoanna, CD, TDI, U-CD, with a new friend she met at a dog show.

Then the dog is left lying down a few paces from the suspect as the handler searches the blind (the bad guy's hiding place). Without warning the suspect runs away, and the dog must attack without command instantly. The dog must release when the suspect gives up. As soon as the dog releases, the suspect attacks the dog, striking it twice with a padded stick. The dog again releases when the suspect gives up. The dog and handler then transport the suspect about 40 paces (the dog and handler walking a few paces behind). The suspect will turn and again attack the handler and again the dog must attack without command and stop the suspect from reaching its handler. The dog is then held by the collar and the courage test is run as in the SchH I. The dog

and handler then transport the suspect to the judge.

Schutzhund Three (SchH III)

SchH III TRACKING: The track is laid by a stranger and must be at least 800 to 1000 paces long, have four right-angle turns with three articles and be aged about one hour.

SchH III OBEDIENCE: Similar to SchH II with the following changes: There is no on-lead heeling. The dog must do two "stand in motion" exercises, one while walking at heel, one while running at heel. The dog is recalled after the running stand. The dog must now retrieve a 4-pound dumbbell on the flat, and must still retrieve over the 39 inch and 6-foot jump. The down stay on the field is also done with the handler out of sight.

SchH III PROTECTION: Similar to SchH II, except distances are greater, and the challenge to the dog greater. After the courage test the dog is again attacked by the suspect and again struck twice with a stick to determine the dog's courage.

Other Schutzhund Titles

Verkehrssichere Begleithunde (Traffic Secure Companion Dog), "B." This is an obedience/temperament test which is for any dog of any breed. It does not require that the dog bite, and when well done, is a very good test of a dog's nerves and stability.

The dog must heel on lead, like in any other Schutzhund trial, and proceed through a group. The dog must then heel off-lead, and will be tested for gunshyness. Then the sit in motion and down in motion exercises and recall will be performed.

Then comes the practical portion of the test. The dog and handler proceed down a street, followed by a judge. The dog will be on a loose lead, and is expected to react with indifference to pedestrians. A jogger passes close by the dog and handler, followed by a bicyclist who will pass very closely from the rear. After that the dog and handler proceed to the judge where they shake hands and engage in conversation. The dog and handler then proceed into an area of very heavy traffic, both human and cars, and the dog must stop and be ordered to lie down once while in the middle of very close traffic.

After that the dog is taken to a quieter area and left tied to a post. A dog is walked past, and the tied dog may not react in an aggressive manner. In the last test the dog is allowed off lead and may roam about. It must respond when called by its owner and come quickly.

THE WATCH DOG TITLE

This title is a test of both the dog's obedience and its ability to protect property. The dog is

A happy bulldog leaves the training field with her toy.

tested in routine obedience including heeling and retrieving. Then the dog is taken to an enclosed area and left. The dog must respond aggressively when a stranger approaches. The stranger flees and proceeds to an area where the dog cannot reach him (such as inside a dog kennel). The dog is quickly released and ordered to pursue the person. The dog must pursue and stop at where the person is hiding, then bark. Then the dog is secured to a runner cable, and must react with aggression when approached from both sides by menacing strangers.

THE AD (ENDURANCE) TEST

Some clubs offer a title for those who ride a bicycle 12 miles with

Tatman's Samson, ACE, SchH III.

An APBT strikes the sleeve with perfect form.

their dog alongside. This is called the endurance test. The problem with this test is that any dog can be forced to run 12 miles regardless of whether he was in proper condition or not. Many people do not properly condition their dogs, and the author has seen dogs complete the AD test with their bleeding feet wrapped in duct tape. This test needs some serious rethinking to be a feasible working degree.

HERDING

The Pit Bull is, technically, a stock dog. Its original name and purpose—Bulldog—indicate that the dog has a long history of working with cattle and bulls. The style of stock work that the Bulldog was developed for is rarely used these days. Dogs which can stop and control a bull are rarely needed except in a few remote range areas. These days the herding and stock dogs are characterized by small agile breeds which have been expressly bred to nip at the stock and move it with as little fuss as possible. Examples are the Australian Cattle Dog, the Kelpie and the Border Collie. These dogs are

(HC) means that the dog has been found to have sufficient instinct to warrant further training. To earn a HC title, the dog is turned loose with stock and its actions are watched by the tester. A dog who attacks or chases stock will be dismissed. Only a dog who exhibits a strong desire to gather up and move

The Pit Bull's original purpose was stock control. Here Lyssa Noble-Stoehm and Petie work sheep.

characteristically quick, agile dogs which survive by being faster than the cow. They dart in and out, nipping, and never taking a hold. Their job is to move stock, not control or hold it.

The strong herding instinct is apparent in many modern Pit Bulls, and several have been tested and "Herding Certified" by the American Herding Breed Association. Herding Certified

stock will be certified. The dogs which enter this certification should have received no prior training, so that what the tester judges is the dog's own instinct.

At one time, herding trials were open to all breeds, traditional and non-traditional, and the attitude was "may the best dog win." Today though, the Australian Shepherd Club of America's trials, the American

Hard-working Beringer working sheep in a dust bowl. Owner, Dan Guerra.

Kennel Club's herding trials and the American Herding Breed Association's trials are generally restricted to all but a few specific breeds (not even all the herding breeds are allowed). This appears to have come about due to pressure from breeders of herding breeds who were uncomfortable with the fact that "non-traditional" herding breeds were winning over "traditional" dogs at trials. The Australian Shepherd Club of America reportedly closed their trials to "non-traditional" breeds as a direct result of the winning ways of a Pit Bull at their trials! When the dog retired, the trials were again opened to some "non-traditional" breeds.

Bandog Dread was the first Bulldog to enter sanctioned herding trials, and he did very well considering he had very little training or experience on stock. He earned sanctioned herding titles through the Australian Shepherd Club of America's herding program, and placed in the ribbons several times. Dread trialed on ducks, sheep and cattle, and it was very disconcerting for the Aussie owners when a Pit Bull passed while their dogs often failed!

The AHBA's herding trials are designed around the sheepdog-type trials, and are not as suitable for a stock dog like an APBT. Bandog Dread has competed in these trials as well though, and earned highest scoring dog in trial on ducks at his last trial!

The purpose of the herding trial is for the dog to move the stock around an area in a set pattern, keeping the stock as quiet and unharried as possible. Persons interested in herding should locate the local herding club or trainers. Be aware that most trainers will want only to work with the traditional breeds they are used to, and you would be better off simply to watch them work their dogs and learn what you can. Most people use ducks, as they are easier to control and keep than sheep.

Herding trials have come under increasing criticism for causing unnecessary trauma to the stock. Generally at any sanctioned trial there will be injuries or even fatalities to one or more of the animals being used. Stronger humane guidelines and strict regulating of show-type dogs who do not possess real instinct and are simply chasing and harassing stock will have to be adopted and enforced if herding is to remain a viable working sport.

CONFORMATION

The word "conformation" means "state of being similar or like," "conforming," and describes the goals of a conformation show. At a conformation show, dogs are judged on how similar they are to the written standard of the breed. The conformation show is what most people think of when they think of a dog show.

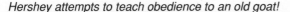

Hershey attempts to teach obedience to an old goat!

Petie does a nice little "out-run" around the sheep. He does a good job of keeping the sheep close to his handler.

Each breed has a written standard of perfection for appearance, and the goal of a show breeder is to produce a dog as close to that standard as possible. Good breeders strive to produce a dog that is sound and mentally stable as well. At a UKC conformation show, dogs of similar age and sex are judged against each other and against the standard, and the best dog of each age and sex group then competes against all the other age and sex groups for the best male, best female and then Best of Breed. Points are awarded for each win, and after a certain amount of points has been won, the dog is considered a "champion."

In United Kennel Club shows, a dog is awarded points for winning each class. For instance, a 14-month-old female would be shown against all other females age 12 to 24 months. If she was chosen as the best in her class, she would receive ten UKC points. If she went on to win Best Female, she would earn 15 more points. When compared to the Best Male, if she were chosen Best of Show, she would receive an additional ten points. It takes 100 points to become a UKC champion, and a dog must win at least one Best Male or Best Female. Unlike the AKC, a dog may be awarded points even if it is the only dog in its class.

In AKC shows, the dog must

AKC Ch./Gr. Ch. Perdue's One Eyed Jack is both an AKC and UKC Champion. He is owned by Pam Perdue and was bred by Ginny York.

obtain 15 AKC points to become a champion. Between one and five points are given at each show, depending on how many dogs are competing. The smaller the number of dogs, the smaller the number of points. A dog must win at least two "majors" (three to five points) in order to finish. There must be at least one other dog competing in order to win points. Points are only awarded to the Winners Dog (or bitch) and then Winners Bitch (and then Best of Winners). Class winners receive no points.

One problem with conformation shows is that many pups are purchased for show purposes only to develop into dogs with faults such as missing teeth or an incorrect tail set. What happens to these dogs? If the owner's only desire was a dog which they could show, the dog might be sold or destroyed, and another bought in its place. It can be frustrating to a puppy owner, who truly loves his dog, to find that no matter how hard he trains or tries, he cannot win. This is not the case in almost any other dog sport, such as obedience, where you and the dog—not the judge—determine whether you win or not.

American conformation shows

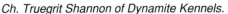
Ch. Truegrit Shannon of Dynamite Kennels.

Ch. Lar-San Deity in the UKC conformation ring.

create another stumbling block to the responsible breeder; the young champion. In both AKC and UKC a dog may be declared a champion in conformation long before his appearance has finalized. When a dog becomes a champion at eight months, no one can tell if his hips will stay strong, if he will go oversize or develop many other faults. These young dogs may also mature into dogs with terrible temperaments—and yet they will already be a champion!

Showing a dog in conformation can be fun, but a championship in what a dog looks like should never be given more importance than it is due. A dog's appearance is probably about the last thing on which a dog should be judged. Soundness

(and there are *plenty* of unsound champions!), good temperament, proper working drives and intelligence are far more important, and these things are judged in the working trial, not the conformation ring. Those wishing to show their dogs in conformation would be well advised to wait until the dog is mature (about 24 months) and has passed OFA, and is well started in obedience work before beginning a show career. And don't worry about obedience "ruining" a dog for the show ring. Some of the most obedience-titled dogs in the country, such as Bandog Dread, One Stone Berek, Gallant Titan and Panda's Gallant Finale, have all earned their championships after obedience training.

This little APBT is competing in a puppy class at UKC show.

A scene from a UKC conformation show. All the dogs are red/red-nose APBTs.

WEIGHT PULLING

The sport of weight pulling was developed as a result of the work of the northern breeds, yet it is an ideal sport for the strong and competitive Bulldog! The sport strikes some people as possibly cruel; you are, after all, asking the dog to pull a heavy weight. The key here is that you are *asking* the dog to pull, and only a dog that enjoys pulling will ever pull well. In any sport in any field, abuses can occur, but the sport of weight pulling as sponsored by the International Weight Pull Association certainly is designed with the dog's enjoyment and protection in mind.

The trick with weight pulling is to understand it—learn as much as you can about it before you actually start training your dog, and understand which organizations work to protect the dog and the sport. If you attend a weight pull or two before you actually go out and start working your dog, you will come to understand why the harnesses are the way they are, and how to tell if a dog is really making an effort or not. You will also learn why it is so important to train at low weights. If, instead, you run right out and buy a walking or tracking harness, or even an ill-fitting pulling harness, hook your dog up to a couple tires and yell "Come 'ere!" at him, you may very well ruin what could have otherwise been an excellent pulling dog.

The only real danger of injury in weight pulling can occur if you allow or even encourage your dog to jerk against the harness, which is what occurs at "baiting contests" held by some organizations under the name of weight pulling. Here the dog is baited (with practically anything) and encouraged to throw itself against the harness in an effort to reach the bait. A dog with strong prey drives, like most APBTs, can injure themselves attempting to reach the bait, and should never be encouraged to jerk. A dog lunging for a bait presents a very different picture from the calm effort put forth by a trained pulling dog. In IWPA pulls, the dog is not allowed sufficient space to get a running start, and is never baited. The dog is encouraged to ease slowly into the harness and pull calmly with his nose to the floor and all his feet on the ground, for this is the style that wins.

The International Weight Pull Association is a non-profit corporation that promotes the sport of weight pulling through organized and sanctioned pulls on either snow with a sled or on the ground with a wheeled cart. The IWPA welcomes dogs of all breeds and mixed breeds. It is truly a sport where "the best dog wins!" regardless of breeding.

The object of a dog pull is to see who has the strongest, best conditioned dog at the pull. The dogs are pulled in different weight groups, so that small dogs don't have to compete directly against large dogs. Smaller dogs generally pull more per body weight than larger dogs though. Classes are 1–35 lbs., 36–60 lbs., 61–80 lbs.,

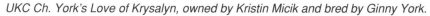

UKC Ch. York's Love of Krysalyn, owned by Kristin Micik and bred by Ginny York.

Carla Restivo and Sagebrush Tacoma Danni, TT, OFA, practice weight pulling in sub-zero temperature.

81–100 lbs., 101–120 lbs. and the "unlimited" class, which is all dogs over 120 pounds.

The dogs start at low weights, pulling the cart 16 feet in 60 seconds. Weight is added in increments, and a handler is allowed up to two passes in a row to keep from tiring his dog at the lower weights. A dog must mind its manners in the holding area, where the dogs that are currently pulling wait for their turn to come up as they are competing. No growling or other aggressive behavior is allowed. There are always several excited dogs in the holding area, and handlers who cannot control their dogs are asked to leave.

The dog is attached to the cart and "lined out" to the end of the line which connects it to the cart. The handler will tell the dog to stay and either go to stand behind the cart if he "drives" the dog, or will go stand across the 16-foot-line if he "calls" the dog. The dog must stay until told to pull; it is only allowed two false starts. When the handler calls or commands the dog to pull, the timekeeper starts the 60-second watch. The handler may not touch the dog, cross the line or bait the dog in any way.

In the event that two dogs pull the same amount of weight, and then can pull no more, the winner is determined by the time. The dog who took the shortest amount of time to pull the weight wins. Prizes are given both for the most weight pulled per class, and also for the most weight pulled per pound of body weight per class. For instance, a dog which weighed only 10 pounds and pulled 400 pounds would be actually a better pulling dog than a 30-pound dog that pulled 500 pounds in the 1-35 lbs. class. That is why the percent per pound award is given.

The IWPA offers three working titles for weight pulling. These titles are based on the dog's ability to pull a certain percent of

Above: An ADBA weight pull, where the dog is "baited" and cart is placed on rails. **Below:** Here the handler walks behind the dog during the pull. This is called "driving" the dog.

its body weight three to four times during the season. Since it is much harder for a dog to pull on snow then on the ground, the weight requirements are much lower for snow pulls. The titles are:

WORKING DOG (WD): 12 times its body weight at least four times.

WORKING DOG EXCELLENT (WDX): 18 times its body weight at least four times.

WORKING DOG SUPERIOR (WDS): 21 times its body weight at least three times.

All percentages given here are for ground pulls; snow pull weights would be lower.

One thing about weight pull— you can never compare the weights you see one dog pulling with the weight pulled at another pull. It is the nature of weight pulling that the conditions, carts and pulling surface will radically affect the amounts pulled. For instance, a 60-pound dog may be able to pull 10,000 pounds at a pull that uses a "trolley" system which involves steel wheels riding on steel rails. This system allows for very high weights with a minimum of effort. This system is not allowed at IWPA pulls, which requires a pulling surface at least 10 feet wide, and the cart must ride on the same surface that the dog pulls on. The same 60-pound dog may be able to pull 3,000 pounds at a very good IWPA pull, with a good chute and a good cart. However, this same 60-pound dog may

This Pit Bull is in advanced weight-pull training, as he drags the tire over rough terrain.

A four-month-old Pit Bull prepares for early Schutzhund work. Here she is getting ready to do some prey work.

Three Am. Staffs bring in one stick!

it doesn't take too many tires to make an extremely heavy load. And unlike wheels, tires don't build up momentum, so the dog must pull hard the whole time, not just when starting the forward movement. You may begin adding weight slowly after that, but remember the secret is to add weight up and take weight down in no particular order so the dog doesn't feel that the weight will always get harder.

There are two main kinds of pullers: those who pull their dogs until they can't pull anymore and they quit, and those who pull for a certain amount and then stop their dogs. The problem with pulling a dog until it quits is that pretty quickly the dog learns that it is always going to become very difficult, and the dog will give up more easily. The safest thing is never to over-pull a young or novice dog. You will be able to tell when it is nearing its limit. If you have trained long and hard at the lower weights, your dog will have developed the best style (because it finds it works for it) and won't be lunging and jerking like the dog that is rushed or baited. What you are looking for is a dog which starts slow, puts its head down, nose to the floor and pulls hard with its front legs while pushing with its back legs.

There is no point in over-pulling dogs. If a dog barely succeeds in pulling a weight, giving its best effort, what is the point in asking it to pull the next weight up? If your dog pulls well, then you have seen what you came to see, no matter what your placement.

him that he can move a load. If you pile on the weight before the dog understands that you will not ask him to move something he cannot, the dog will lose faith and give up easily. The first few weeks the dog will simply be learning to accept the harness, to stay when left, and to come to you against the slight pull of the easy weight. Don't ask the dog to pull the tire all over the yard. Keep the distance to 20 feet each pull, and make a *huge* fuss when the dog gets to you, petting, praising and giving him a tidbit if you like.

Just doing this for two weeks may seem boring, but you are building in the dog's mind the strong belief that, whenever you call "Hike!", "Dig!" or "Pull!" to him, he can do it, and it is fun!

Now after two weeks you can add a little weight in the form of a second tire. Because of their drag,

CONDITIONING

It sure helps to have your pulling dog in top condition. Stamina is important as he will be pulling several times in a row. Of course powerful muscles are important also, and the best form of conditioning for the pulling dog is a mile or so walk each evening dragging a light tire. The weight should not be much—it is the constant slight resistance which builds stamina. Overloading the dog nightly will only tear muscle tissue down. Better to increase the distance of the walk than the weight of the drag.

Weight pulling is fun, the dogs enjoy it, and it builds a bond between dog and handler as only work can do.

FRISBEE

If you have a large backyard, a Bulldog, and a Frisbee®, you have the recipe for a great time! Pit Bulls are natural frisbee dogs, having a strong prey drive and athletic body suitable for fancy catches in mid-air. Some cities even offer frisbee-catching contests for dogs.

To get a dog interested in a frisbee, show it to the dog and

Ch. Spartan's Zoanna U-CD, PR Timberline's Humbug U-CD, and PR Timberline's Maggie U-CD, take a break during training.

then roll it away from it a few times. Act excited and grab the frisbee away from it, acting as if it is a game of keep-away. Try to race the dog to it and snatch it away from him. If he wants to chase it, toss it lightly at head level until the dog gets the idea of taking it from the air. If he shows little interest, continue to roll the frisbee away from him five or six times a day while you chase after it. The dog will soon want the toy that you find so exciting.

Nylabone® products offers a wide array of flying discs designed especially for active dogs. For Bulldogs, only the largest and hardest nylon discs can be recommended—these are called Nylabone® Frisbees®.

SPRINGPOLE

A springpole is any device which allows the dog to play tug-o-war with himself. Most commonly it is a piece of burlap tied to a spring which is attached to a tree limb. Sometimes, where there is an absence of trees, a stand is made for the spring. The idea is to attach a biting surface to a spring and attach that to some firm object overhead. The dog is introduced to the springpole much like a frisbee. Keep the biting surface head high, jerk it around, pat it, and act

Pit Bulls love to play in the snow. Here, Bandog Bad prepares to blast off after a flying disc.

Diane Jessup prepares Gr. Ch. Guerra's Beringer for Schutzhund work by introducing him to the springpole. She taps the rag lightly to encourage him.

excited about it. If the dog grasps it, praise him, and keep a steady, even side-to-side motion on the rope between the spring and the biting surface. Some dogs will instantly grasp the idea of the springpole. A few never care for the idea at all. It is important not to allow the dog to play on the springpole for too long—he will lose interest. It is best to keep the sessions to no longer than ten minutes.

Some dogs enjoy leaping and grasping a springpole which is suspended in the air. This really is enjoyable for many dogs, and while there is a slight risk of injury from this "sport," most dogs play springpole all their lives

Above: Two APBTs make jumping look easy. *Below:* Cindy Lottinville's Lulu Belle showing fine form in an agility trial.

Above: A Pit Bull negotiating the sway-bridge. **Below:** *Pit Bull dashing back to her owner in flyball competition.*

Association and the National Club of Dog Agility. Dog owners interested in the sport should contact local trainers to find a club in their area. Virginia Isaac, of Sacramento, California, is one Pit Bull owner who has become very active in agility training. She has developed a course called the "challenge course," which features extremely challenging pieces, including a ten-foot tower which the dog must climb alone! Virginia's dog Sam was the first agility-titled Pit Bull. Even at ten years of age he is still putting on demonstrations in challenge course agility, showcasing the breed's grit and gameness in yet another fashion.

YOUR OWN PERSONAL GAME!

One of the great things about owning Pit Bulldogs is that they are just so much fun! You and your own dog can think up your own games to play together. Pit Bulldogs run on scent hurdle teams, and others play tug-o-war with tug toys especially designed for the purpose. With a Bulldog beside you, you have the best companion imaginable for work or play.

The all-American dog, the American Pit Bull Terrier. Owner, Virginia Isaac.

An APBT flies through the tire on an agility course.

Left: A Tacoma-bred dog shows his outstanding prey drive by his intense play with the hose. This dog can do any work. ***Below:*** Cindy Lottinville's Daisy Mae makes a great catch.

York's Cherub U-CD, UKC-registered APBT doing a jump in style.

Today's Pit Bulldog

Among the many myths surrounding this breed, one of the most enduring and yet most inaccurate is that the majority, or a large percentage, of Pit Bulls are bred and maintained as fighting dogs. As many states passed felony dog fighting laws, a few southwestern states (notably Utah and Arizona) became the gathering place of "professional fighters." In these places, along with some areas of the south and midwest, there are pockets of fighters; and there are certainly people who "roll" their dogs in every state or large town. However, only a small fraction of the APBTs born today are ever intentionally fought.

*At left: By earning more training titles than any other dog, Bandog Dread has proven that the APBT is the most versatile breed. **Below:** UKC-registered "Roxy," owned by John Froome, is a Geroux-Ruffian breeding.*

Above: York's Valentine, whose coloring is called tri-colored or brindle point. **Below:** "Diego," owned by Dan Schwarzle, is an AKC/ UKC-registered Pit Bull of Estrella lines.

Today's Bulldog is kept primarily as a pet, usually selected by people who have come to know the breed through dogs kept by friends or family members. In this age of unhealthy and shy purebreds, the Pit Bull is unique indeed in that a large portion of its population is still unspoiled by show breeding and remains healthy and friendly. Hip dysplasia does occur in the breed and will become an increasing problem as breeders intermix American Staffordshire lines, some of which are riddled with dysplasia, into Pit Bulldog lines. But as yet it is still possible to find lines with low incidence of this disease.

Today's Pit Bull owners are finding that their dogs are certainly as versatile as any breed, and indeed, an APBT holds

York's Blue Angel, an AKC/UKC registered bitch owned by Ruth Teeter.

the title of the world's most versatile dog (holding training titles in more areas than any other dog of any other breed). As we have seen in the pages of this book, it is not uncommon to see a Pit Bulldog winning "high in trial" at all-breed obedience trials or winning at a weight-pulling contest. APBTs have earned "highest scoring dog" at all-breed herding trials, and have excelled at tracking trials. Several dozen Pit Bulls have competed in the complex sport of Schutzhund, the most exacting of working-dog sports, and they have commonly won "high in trial" awards at

Today the APBT is loved as a working dog, show dog, and family pet. Owners, Ervin and Becky Gross.

these civilian police-dog trials. We've seen that many APBTs are currently registered as therapy dogs who are helping to spread goodwill and happiness to many elderly people living in retirement and convalescent homes. Some dogs visit hospitals for children. There are Pit Bulls working as certified Search and Rescue dogs. APBTs are helping to locate drugs for both private narcotics detectors and as detector dogs for the US government. There doesn't seem to be much the APBT is not capable of doing or learning, and

the future of this unspoiled working breed looks secure as a competition training/sport dog, hunting dog, and faithful family watchdog and companion.

All over America, more than half a million Pit Bulldogs are kept as pets. These dogs represent no greater threat to the public than any other population of dogs and they need not be afforded any special treatment. There are a few dogs maintained and trained for violent purposes such as guarding illegal narcotics or pit fighting, but these poor animals are a small minority and an entire breed cannot be judged by the actions of these few irresponsibe owners. No matter how spectacular the actions of these few may be made to appear in the press, the reality of the numbers remain—the majority of Pit Bulldogs are trustworthy, gentle pets when owned by responsible people.

All through history the rugged Bulldog has attracted a wide variety of fans. Some have exploited his courage and power, using him to overpower animals many times his size. From this task he never shrank. Some have used him as a family protector and this he has done through the ages, protecting against wild animals and marauding humans. Some have been attracted to his intelligence, courage and good nature, keeping him as mascot and companion, and this too he has done with distinction. Some have used him as a working dog, and he has always given his best. The working Bulldog is a natural

PR Ch. Ewing's Morgan, U-CD, a versatile working Pit Bulldog.

wonder, and a treasure indeed that has been handed down throughout the ages to us. What other animal has been so honored as to have his very name be the symbol of courage and gumption around the world? What other animal so stirs the heart and demands respect and admiration from all who see his spirit in action? He is a living legend, a symbol of English courage and pride that has remained pure through the ages. Yet he remains also a humble fellow at heart, and trots along behind his beloved

Riverrun's Coming Up Roses, owned by Ruth Teeter, is shown here working to get donations for the Canine Defense Fund.

Bandog Dread and McGruff the Crime Dog compare dog licenses.

master come fair or foul. He is truly a dog to be proud of in any company, and it remains for today's fanciers to preserve this dog in all its glory. Dog fighters do this breed a great disservice. To waste such a dog on such a senseless and destructive pastime is unforgivable. Today's fancier will help the rugged little Bulldog adjust to the pressures of urban living and find new useful work for him to do. The Bulldog of the future will be working to find trapped people in earthquake rubble, pulling a wheelchair-bound owner, sniffing out narcotics for the government and taking part in tea parties with his owner's toddlers. The jobs may change somewhat, but the Bulldog's great heart and capacity to help mankind will not.

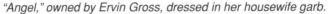

"Angel," owned by Ervin Gross, dressed in her housewife garb.

Private Gidra, U-CD, plays cowboy atop Zeb, a 30-year-old Appaloosa. Owners, Mike and Bobbie Morehouse.

How much are those doggies in the window? APBTs all owned by Ginny York.

Above: *A Pit Bull pup works the flyball machine.*

Below left: *Dan Guerra and Gr. Ch. Guerra's Beringer U-CD, win a costume contest.* ***Below right:*** *AKC Ch. Rowdytown Zaca Consionne, owned by Rich Monske, is dressed as a Poodle for Halloween.*

Above: Gr. Ch.Tyee's Boy Bosworth takes a dip. **Below:** *This Pit Bull couple is all dressed up with nowhere to go.*

The author, Diane Jessup, with Bandog Dread.

"An Old Pit Bulldog Thinks of Death"

When they ask you, if I died well,
Tell them then, the Bulldog's tale;
A tale of courage, dogs bred bold,
A tale of my kind, centuries old.

My blood comes from an ancient age;
Was valued more than king or sage,
Sires and dams of courage rare –
Who took on all who thought to dare.

In my blood flows images of ancient kin,
Of silent stone circles, of small dark men,
I see a savage beast in the flickering light
That those before me stood there to fight.

Rough British bulls go through my sleep,
I hold them fast with courage deep;
I hold them fast for my master's blow
With pride—I hold their noses low.

Before that even, we held the boar,
From those rough dogs comes my core.
We've hunted, guarded, protected and fought—
We've done whatever man has taught.

So never think I would forsake these things
When soon my spirit takes to wings
And when they ask you how I died,
Say, "As a Bulldog—with courage and pride."

Diane Jessup 2/93
Dedicated to Bandog Dread

What creature that, so fierce so bold
That springs and scorns to leave his hold?
It is the Bulldog, matchless, brave—
Like Briton, on the swelling wave.

Pierce Egan

Above: An APBT scales the wall obstacle. *Below:* "Sam," a ten-year-old Pit Bull owned by Virginia Isaac, looks down from the top of the tower on the challenge ability course.

Above: Petie showing the form that made him one of Southern California's top agility dogs.
Below: An APBT walks on the seesaw.

Above left: Great shot of a Pit Bull in action, Chillum Kashari. *Above right:* A beautiful APBT in an animal shelter. *Below:* Ch. Guerra's Beringer U-CD, cools off in the summer heat.

Above: An APBT goes over the hump of a scaling wall. *Below:* This Pit Bull shows the breed's adaptability to all weather conditions.

Left: The symbol of courage and pride around the world; the Pit Bulldog and the gamecock. Both of these noble species have been abused and misunderstood by both those who would fight them and the humane societies which "rescue" them. It is a rare Pit Bull or gamecock which falls into the hands of a person who will love, understand, and not exploit them. ***Below:*** The beautiful and talented "Dolly" owned by Mr. W. Walker of England takes a break during running an agility course. She is a Staffordshire Bull Terrier.

Right: Ch. U-CD, Baroness Copper Bit, BH, owned by Annetta Cheek models a t-shirt made for dogs. This bitch was staying with the author for Schutzhund training and quickly became one of her favorite dogs. Photo by Joyce Marks. *Below:* A lovely Staffordshire Bull bitch and a Border Terrier pictured in England on the bank of the Thames River. This photo clearly illustrates the similarities between these breed cousins.

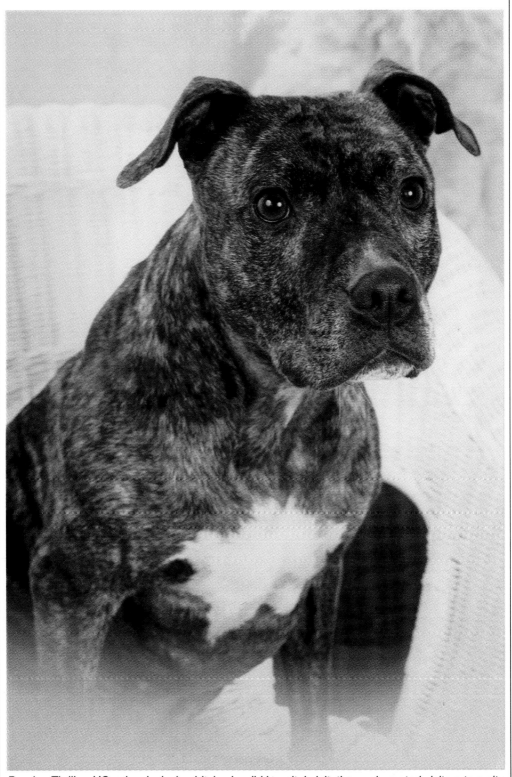

Bandog Thriller, HC, a lovely, loving bitch who did hospital visitation and greeted visitors to a city animal control center for several years.

Epilogue: Why I Call Them "Pit Bulldogs"

There is no breed in the world that has more controversy over its breed name than the dog registered by the United Kennel Club as the "American Pit Bull Terrier." In the text of this book, I have described why this particular name is so inaccurate. This breed is made up of primarily original Bulldog blood, with some terrier infusion. Most, if not all, modern dog breeds were produced by a mixture of dog breeds. However, most breeds will favor one of their basic components more

Leri Hansen's puppy begins tracking training.

Nine-month-old Grip, owned by the author, does a "courage test" as required in Schutzhund competition.

"Arrow," a bitch owned by Charlie Holland, shows beautiful natural ears and nice conformation.

than another. In the case of the pit bull, there is *no doubt* that he shows little terrier characteristics. Therefore, he properly belongs in the bulldog family. Today pit bulls still compete in "catch dog" contests where they grip cattle or hogs. They do not compete in terrier "go to ground" contests.

Terriers are characteristic by generally having rough or broken hair and a very straight front; they are not brindle, pied, or other colors of the Bulldog family; they have small size and, most importantly, as their name "terra" implies, they were developed strictly to go to earth after rodents. Terriers tend to snap at and shake their prey and were traditionally pitted in such a way that the dog which quickly killed the most rats was

Soviet's Deltz takes a break to view the world from the couch.

the winner. Certainly terriers were not bred to grip and hold tenaciously. They are apt to be alert, noisy and suspicious of strangers.

The Bulldog family, on the other hand, is characteristic by medium size, short hair, brindle, fawn, solid or pied coloration, and have been developed for gripping and holding stock. They tend to grab and hold calmly.

They are calm, generally not suspicious of strangers, and rarely noisy.

There are many names which the breed could be called, but I think, after weighing up the facts of terrier versus bulldog, that I do not see the terrier in the better specimens of this breed, and I consider it an honor to continue to call them after their traditional name—Bulldog.

Rip finds a new use for a tire swing. He's six feet off the ground!

Appendix: Titles for the Working Pit Bull

AKC TITLES

Conformation:

Ch.   Champion

Obedience:

CD   Companion Dog
CDX   Companion Dog Excellent

TD   Tracking Dog
TDX   Tracking Dog Excellent
OTCh.   Obedience Trial Champion
UD   Utility Dog
UDX   Utility Dog Excellent
UDT   Utility Dog Tracker (achieved both UD and TD)
UDTX   Utility Dog Tracker Excellent (achieved both UD
               and TDX)

Herding:

STD-d   Started Trial Dog - ducks
STD-s   Started Trial Dog - sheep
HTD-1   Herding Trial Dog
HT   Herding Tested
PT   Pre-trial Tested
HS   Herding Started
HI   Herding Intermediate
HX   Herding Excellent
HCh.   Herding Champion

UKC TITLES

Conformation:

Ch.   Champion
Gr. Ch.   Grand Champion

Obedience:

U-CD   United-Companion Dog
U-CDX   United-Companion Dog Excellent
U-UD   United-Utility Dog

SCHUTZHUND TITLES

*B	Traffic-sure companion dog (formerly BH)
*FH	*Fahrtenhund* (Advanced tracking dog)
WH	*Wachhund* (Watch dog): obedience/guard work/no bitework
SchH A	Schutzhund A: obedience/bitework
SchH I	Schutzhund One: tracking/obedience/bitework
SchH II	Schutzhund Two: intermediate tracking/obedience bitework
SchH III	Schutzhund Three: advanced tracking/obedience bitework
IPO	International Police Exam One: tracking/obedience bitework
IPO II	International Police Exam Two: tracking/obedience bitework
IPO III	International Police Exam Three: tracking/obedience bitework
AD	Endurance test (12 mile run)
*PH	*Polizeihund* (Police dog)

* denotes German title

WEIGHT-PULLING TITLES

WD	Working Dog (IWPA)
WDX	Working Dog Excellent (IWPA)
WDS	Working Dog Superior (IWPA)
ACE	Weight-pulling title (ADBA)

AGILITY TITLES

AD	Agility Dog
AAD	Advanced Agility Dog
MAD	Master Agility Dog

OTHER TITLES

OFA	Orthopedic Foundation for Animals (hip rating: fair, good, or excellent)
TT	Temperament Tested
CGC	Canine Good Citizen
HC	Herding Certified (dog shows aptitude, not training)
SAR	Search and Rescue dog
TDI	Therapy Dog International

Index

Page numbers in **boldface** refer to illustrations.
All titles have been omitted from dogs' names for the reader's convenience.

TS-205, 156 pp.
Over 130 color photos.

TS-220, 64 pp.

TS-212, 256 pp.
Over 140 color photos.

TS-220, 64 pp.